Intentionally blank as was the original edition.

Plate I.

1895.
LILIENTHAL'S LATEST AIRSAILER.

The
Aeronautical
Annual

1896

DEVOTED TO THE ADVANCEMENT OF THE NEGLECTED
SCIENCE

EDITED BY

JAMES MEANS

Aeronautical Publishers
American Aeronautical Archives
One Oakglade Circle • Hummelstown, PA 17036
www.AeronauticalPublishers.com

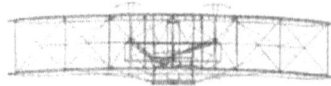

American Aeronautical Archives

Foreword and back cover copyright ©2015
by Mike and Marjie Markowski
All rights reserved under Pan American and
Int'l Copyright Conventions

Published by Markowski International Publishers
One Oakglade Circle, Hummelstown, PA 17036
American Aeronautical Archives is an imprint of
Markowski International Publishers
www.AeronauticalPublishers.com

This Markowski edition is an unabridged facsimile of the original work,
compiled and edited by James Means, and first published in 1896 then in
2003 in Celebration of the Centennial of Flight. It includes all the original
aeronautical photographs and illustrations. The Foreword to the Markowski
Edition was specially prepared for this edition.

Publisher's Cataloguing-in-Publication

Means, James, Editor, 1853-1920
    The Aeronautical Annual 1896: Foreword by Michael A. Markowski, p.cm.
    Originally published in Boston, Massachusetts by W.B. Clarke & Co., 1896
    ISBN: 978-0-938716-96-9

    1.   Flying Machine—History.   2. Aeronautics—History
    I.   Title

Manufactured in the United States of America

THE profits of this edition of THE ANNUAL — if any — will be given to the Boston Aeronautical Society to be added to its Experiment Fund. (See page 86.)

FOREWORD

The *Aeronautical Annuals* of 1895-96-97 are among the most important pre-Wright era aviation books ever published. Prized by collectors, original editions are extremely rare; a pristine original set could be worth $3,000. In tribute to the brave early aviation pioneers, I am delighted to re-publish these treasures and make them available to everyone.

In a letter to James Means's son, Philip, dated November 12, 1921, Orville Wright wrote: "*The Aeronautical Annuals* of 1895-96-97 contained the best collection of reprints from the work of the earlier experimenters in aviation..., and I do not know of a better collection today. Your father showed rare good judgment in his selections, separating most of the good work from the mass of worthless matter which had been published.

"Your father's work was of great benefit to us, and I think of my personal acquaintance with him with affection."

After stumbling upon an original set of these amazing books in 1972 in an old, out-of-the-way bookstore in Boston, with Tom Peghiny, my first student and true friend ever since, I committed to advancing ultralight aviation. Tom went on to become a world champion hangglider pilot, maker of ultralight aircraft, and founder of light sport aircraft leader Flight Design USA. These three books, along with Otto Lilienthal's landmark *Birdflight as the Basis of Aviation*, inspired me to leave my job as an aerospace engineer to design and manufacture hanggliders. I then wrote *The Hang Glider's Bible*, and started publishing books.

In 1899 the Smithsonian recommended the *Annuals* to Wilbur Wright when he wrote asking for information on human flight. These three volumes are books of vision, featuring the plans, dreams, and schemes of some of aviation's visionaries—Da Vinci, Cayley, Henson, Langley, Maxim, Herring, Chanute, Lilienthal, and others.

The *Annuals* provided the Wrights with a wealth of knowledge about the thinking and experiments which had been done up until that time, giving them a foundation on which to formulate their own ideas. Each volume is packed with incredible information, drawings, and photographs of the pre-Wright era, making them must-reads for all aviation enthusiasts.

Blue skies and gentle breezes,
— *Mike Markowski*

CONTENTS.

LIST OF PLATES.

PRACTICAL EXPERIMENTS FOR THE DEVELOP-
MENT OF HUMAN FLIGHT.

By Otto Lilienthal.

(Written expressly for the. Annual.)

WHOEVER has followed with attention the technical treatises on flying will have become convinced that human flight cannot be brought about by one single invention, but is proceeding towards its perfection by a gradual development; for only those trials have met with success which correspond with such a development.

Formerly men sought to construct flying machines in a complete form, at once capable of solving the problem, but gradually the conviction came that our physical and technical knowledge and our practical experiences were by far insufficient to overcome a mechanical task of such magnitude without more preliminaries.

Those proceeding on this basis therefore applied themselves, not to the problem of flying as a whole, but rather divided it into its elements, and sought first to bring a clear understanding into said elements which should form the basis of final success. For example, take the laws of atmospheric resistance, upon which all flying depends, and regarding which, until very recent years, the greatest uncertainty has existed; these have now been defined to such an extent that the different phases of flight can be treated mathematically. Besides which, the physical processes of the natural flight of the creatures have become the subject of minute investigation, and have in most cases been satisfactorily explained. The nature of the wind also, and its influence on flying bodies, have been carefully studied, thus enabling us to understand several peculiarities of the birds' flight hitherto unexplainable, so that one can apply the results thus obtained in perfecting human flight.

The theoretical apparatus needed for the technics of flying has been enriched so much by all these studies within the last few years that the elements of flying apparatus can now be calculated and constructed with sufficient accuracy. By means of this theoretical knowledge one is enabled to form and construct wing- and sailing-surfaces according as the intended effect renders it desirable.

But with all this, we are not yet capable of constructing and using complete flying machines which answer all requirements. Being desirous of furthering with all speed the solution of the problem of flight, men have repeatedly formed projects in these last few years which represent complete air-ships moved by dynamos; but the constructors are not aware of the difficulties which await us as soon as we approach the realizing of any ideas in flying.

All those, who have occupied themselves to any extent with actual flying experiments, have found that, even if they mastered theoretically the problem of flying, the practical solving of the same can only be brought about by a gradual and wearisome series of experiments based one upon the other.

Also the practical tasks of the technics of flying should be simplified and divided as much as possible instead of steering straight to the final goal.

As these principles have been seldom carried out, the practical results in human flight have remained very scanty up to the present day.

One can get a proper insight into the practice of flying only by actual flying experiments. The journey in the air without the use of the balloon is absolutely necessary in order to gain a judgment as to the actual requirements for an independent flight. It is in the air itself that we have to develop our knowledge of the stability of flight so that a safe and sure passage through the air may be obtained, and that one can finally land without destroying the apparatus. One must gain the knowledge and the capacity needed for these things before he can occupy himself successfully with practical flying experiments.

As a rule the projectors and constructors of flying machines have not gathered this absolutely necessary practical experience, and have therefore wasted their efforts upon complicated and costly projects.

In free flight through the air a great many peculiar phenomena take place which the constructor never meets with elsewhere; in particular, those of the wind must be taken into consideration in the construction and in the employment of flying apparatus. The manner in which we have to meet the irregularities of the wind when soaring in the air can only be learnt by being in the air itself. At the same time it must be considered that one single blast of wind can destroy the apparatus and even the life of the person flying. This danger can only be avoided by becoming acquainted with the wind by constant and regular practice and by perfecting the apparatus so that we may achieve safe flight.

The only way which leads us to a quick development in human flight is a systematic and energetic practice in actual flying experiments. These experiments and exercises in flying must not only be carried out by scientists, but should also be practised by those wishing for an exciting amusement in the open air, so that the apparatus and the way of using it may by means of common use be quickly brought to the highest possible degree of perfection.

The question is therefore to find a method by which experiments in flying may be made without danger, and may at the same time be indulged in as an interesting amusement by sport-loving men.

Another condition is, that simple, easily constructed, and cheap apparatus should be used for such flying exercises, in order to conduce to a still more general participation in this sport.

All these conditions are easily fulfilled. One can fly long distances with quite simple apparatus without taxing one's strength at all, and this kind of free and safe motion through the air affords greater pleasure than any other kind of sport.

From a raised starting point, particularly from the top of a flat hill, one can, after some practice, soar through the air, reaching the earth only after having gone a great distance.

For this purpose I have hitherto employed a sailing apparatus very like the outspread pinions of a soaring bird. The drawings opposite page 22 represent such apparatus. It consists of a wooden frame covered with shirting (cotton-twill). The frame is taken hold of by the hands, the arms resting between cushions, thus supporting the body. The legs remain free for running and jumping. The steering in the air is brought about by changing the centre of gravity. This apparatus I had constructed with supporting surfaces of ten to twenty square metres. The larger sailing surfaces move in an incline of one to eight, so that one is enabled to fly eight times as far as the starting hill is high. The steering is facilitated by the rudder, which is firmly fastened behind in a horizontal and vertical position.

The machines weigh, according to their size, from 15 to 25 kilograms (33 to 55 lbs.).

In order to practise flying with these sailing surfaces one first takes short jumps on a somewhat inclined surface till he has accustomed himself to be borne by the air. Finally, he is able to sail over inclined surfaces as far as he wishes.

The supporting capacity of the air is felt, particularly if there is a breeze. A sudden increase in the wind causes a longer stoppage in the air, or one is raised to a still higher point.

The charm of such flight is indescribable, and there could not be a healthier motion or more exciting sport in the open air.

The rivalry in these exercises cannot but lead to a constant perfecting of the apparatus, the same as, for instance, is the case with bicycles. I speak from experience, for, although the system of my sailing apparatus remains the same, it has gone through numberless changes from year to year.[1]

The apparatus which I now employ for my flying exercises

---

[1] See article entitled " Wheeling and Flying."

contains a great many improvements as compared with the first
sailing surfaces with which I commenced this kind of experiment five years ago.   The first attempts in windy weather
taught me that suitable steering surfaces would be needed to
enable me to keep my course better against the wind.   Repeated changes in the construction led to a kind of apparatus
with which one can throw himself without danger from any
height, reaching the earth safely after a long distance.   The
construction of the machine is such that it resembles in all its
parts a strut-frame, the joints of which are calculated to stand
pull and pressure, in order to combine the greatest strength with
the least weight.

An important improvement was to arrange the apparatus for
folding which can be seen the most clearly in the figure opposite page 22.   All of my recent machines are so arranged that
they can be taken through a door 2 metres high.   The unfold-
ing and putting together of the flying implements takes about
two minutes.

A single grip of the hands is sufficient to attach the apparatus
safely to the body, and one gets out of the apparatus just as
quickly on landing. , In case of a storm the flying-sail is folded up
in half a minute and can be laid by anywhere.   If one should not
care to fold the apparatus, he may await the end of the storm
under cover of the wings, which are capable of protecting twenty
persons.   Even the heaviest rain will not damage the apparatus.
The flying apparatus, even if completely drenched, is soon
dried by a few sailing flights after the rain stops, as the air
passes through the same with great speed.

The latest improvements of the flying apparatus which I use
for practical experiments refer to gaining of greater stability in
windy weather.

My experiments tend particularly in two directions.   On the
one side I endeavor to carry my experiments in sailing
through the air with immovable wings to this extent; I practise
the overcoming of the wind in order to penetrate, if possible,
into the secret of continued soaring flight.   On the other hand
I try to attain the dynamic flight by means of flapping the

wings, which are introduced as a simple addition to my sailing flights. The mechanical contrivances necessary for the latter, which can reach a certain perfection only by gradual development, do not allow yet of my making known any definite results. But I may state that since my sailing flights of last summer, I am on much more intimate terms with the wind.

What has prevented me till now from using winds of any strength for my sailing experiments, has been the danger of a violent fall through the air, if I should not succeed in retaining the apparatus in those positions by which one insures a gentle landing. The wildly rushing wind tries to dash about the free-floating body, and if the apparatus take up a position, if only for a short time, in which the wind strikes the flying surfaces from above, the flying body shoots downward like an arrow, and can be smashed to pieces before one succeeds in attaining a more favorable position in which the wind exercises a supporting effect. The stronger the wind blows, the easier this danger occurs, as the gusts of wind are so much the more irregular and violent.

As long as the commotion of the air is but slight, one does not require much practice to go quite long distances without danger. But the practice with strong winds is interesting and instructive, because one is at times supported quite by the wind alone. The size of the apparatus, however, unhappily limits us. We may not span the sailing-surfaces beyond a certain measure, if we do not wish to make it impossible to manage them in gusty weather. If the surfaces of 14 square metres [1] do not measure more than 7 metres [2] from point to point, we can eventually overcome moderate winds of about 7 metres [3] velocity, provided one is well practised. With an apparatus of this size it has happened to me that a sudden increase in the wind has taken me way up out of the usual course of flying, and has sometimes kept me for several seconds at one point of the air. It has happened in such a case, that I have been lifted vertically by a gust of wind from the top of the hill (shown in Fig. 3), floating for a time above the same at a height of about 5 metres, whence I then continued my flight, against the wind.

---

[1] About 150 sq. feet.   [2] About 23 feet.   [3] About 22 miles per hour.

Although, while making these experiments I was thrown about by the wind quite violently and was made to execute quite a dance in the air in order to keep my balance, I yet was always enabled to effect a safe landing, but still I came to the conviction, that an increase in the size of the wings or the utilizing of still stronger winds which would lengthen the journey in the air, would necessitate something being done, to perfect the steering and to facilitate the management of the apparatus. This appeared to me to be all the more important as it is very necessary for the development of human flight that all, who take up such experiments, should quickly learn how to use the apparatus safely and understand how to use the same even if the air is disturbed. It is in the wind that this practice becomes so exciting and bears the character of a sport, for all the flights differ from each other and the adroitness of the sailing-man has the largest field for showing itself. Courage also and decision can be here shown in a high degree.

If such exercises are gone through with in a regular and approved method, they are not more dangerous than if one engages in riding, or sailing on the water.

Just as it is in sports on the water, so it is in sports in the air, that the greatest aim will be to reach the most startling results. The machines themselves, as well as the adroitness of their operators, will vie with each other.

He who succeeds in flying the farthest from a certain starting-point, will come forth from the contest as conqueror. This fact will necessarily lead to the production of more and more improved flying apparatus. In a short time we shall have improvements of which to-day we have not the faintest idea.

The foundation for such a development exists already; it only needs a more thorough carrying out to gain perfection. The greater the number is of such persons who have the furthering of flying and the perfecting of the flying apparatus at heart the quicker we shall succeed in reaching a perfect flight. It is therefore of paramount importance that as many physically and technically well-trained men as possible take interest in these

affairs, and that an apparatus be constructed which is as convenient and as cheap as possible.

The means by which I sought to facilitate the management of
the machines and to increase their use in wind, consisted in the
first place in different arrangements for changing the shape of
the wings at will. I will, however, pass over the results here
obtained as another principle gave surprisingly favorable results.

My experiments in sailing flight have accustomed me to
bring about the steering by simply changing the centre of
gravity.

The smaller the surface extension of the apparatus is, the
better control I have over it, and yet if I employ smaller bearing
surfaces in stronger winds, the results are not more favorable.
The idea therefore occurred to me to apply two smaller surfaces,
one above the other, which both have a lifting effect when sailing through the air. Thus the same result must follow which

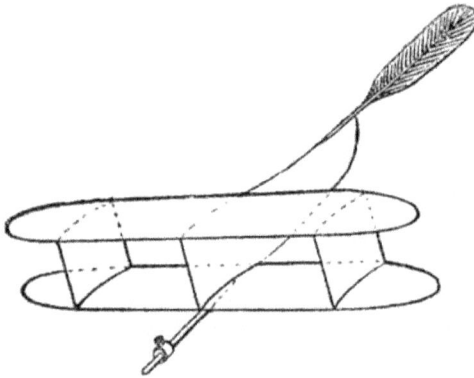

FIG. 1.

would be gained by a single surface of twice the bearing
capacity, but on account of its small dimensions this apparatus
obeys much better the changes of the centre of gravity.

Before I proceeded to construct these double-sailing machines,
I made small models in paper after that system, in order to
study the free movements in the air of such flying bodies and
then to construct my apparatus on a large scale, depending on

Plate II.

Fig. 3.

Fig. 4.

Intentionally blank as was the original edition.

the results thus obtained. The very first experiments with these small models, the form of which may be seen in Figs. I

Fig 2.

and 2, surprised me greatly on account of the stability of their flight. It appears as if the arrangement of having one surface over the other had materially increased the safety and uniformity of the flight. As a rule it is rather difficult to produce models resembling birds, which, left to themselves, glide through the air from a higher point in uniformly inclined lines. I need only recall the extensive and expensive experiments made by Messrs. Riedinger, von Sigsfeld, and von Parsefal, of Augsburg, which showed the difficulty of constructing models that would automatically take up a course of stable flight. I myself doubted formerly very much that an inanimate body sailing quickly forward, could be well balanced in the air, and was all the better pleased in succeeding in this with my little double surfaces.

Relying on this experience I constructed first a double apparatus (Fig. 3), in which each surface contains 9 square metres.[1] I thus produced a comparatively large bearing surface of 18 square metres with but 5½ metres [2] span.

The upper surface is separated from the lower by a distance equal to three quarters of the breadth of the lower surface, and it has no disturbing influence whatever, but creates only a vertically acting lifting force. One must consider that with such an apparatus one always cuts the air quickly, so that both surfaces are met by the air-current, and therefore both act as lifters.

The whole management of such an apparatus is just the same as that of a single sailing surface. I could, therefore, use at once the skill I had already obtained.

Fig. 4 shows how I have to change the centre of gravity, and

---

[1] About 97 sq. feet.   [2] About 18 feet.

particularly the position of the legs, to the left, in order to press down the left wing, which is a little raised. In Fig. 5 the opposite movement to the right is shown. I retain the middle position, as shown in the frontispiece, whenever the apparatus floats horizontally.

The flights undertaken with such double sailing surfaces are distinguished by their great height, as is shown in Fig. 6, which gives a side-view of the apparatus.

The landing with this apparatus is brought about in the same way as with the single sailing surfaces by raising the apparatus in front somewhat and by lessening the speed, as shown in Fig. 7.

Fig. 8 shows an exact picture of the construction of the apparatus, as well as of the management of the same.

The energetic effect of the change of the centre of gravity and the safe starting of the apparatus obtained by it gave me courage to trust myself to a wind which at times exceeded a velocity of 10 metres (about 24 miles per hour).

This gave the most interesting results of all my practical flying experiments hitherto. Six or seven metres velocity of wind sufficed to enable the sailing surface of 18 square metres to carry me almost horizontally against the wind from the top of my hill without any starting jump. If the wind is stronger, I allow myself to be simply lifted from the point of the hill and to sail slowly towards the wind. The direction of the flight has, with strong wind, a strong upward tendency. I often reach positions in the air which are much higher than my starting-point. At the climax of such a line of flight I sometimes come to a standstill for some time, so that I am enabled while floating to speak with the gentlemen who wish to photograph me, regarding the best position for the photographing.[1]

At such times I feel plainly that I would remain floating if I leaned a little towards one side, described a circle and proceeded with the wind. The wind itself tends to bring this motion about, for my chief occupation in the air consists in preventing

[1] The photographs were made by Drs. Neuhaus and Fülleborn, who used a camera constructed by Dr. Neuhaus on the Stegemann principle.

Plate III.

Fig. 5.

Fig. 6.

Intentionally blank as was the original edition.

a turn either to right or the left, and I know that the hill from which I started lies behind and underneath me, and that I might come into rough contact with it if I attempted circling. My endeavors tend therefore to remove myself farther from the hill either by increased wind or by flapping with the wings, so that I can follow the strongly lifting air-current in a circle, and so that I can have a sufficient space of air under and beside me to succeed in describing with safety a circling flight and to land finally steering against the wind.

As soon as I or any other experimenter succeeds in describing the first circling flight, one may regard this event as one of the most important conquests on the road to perfect flight. From this moment only, one is enabled to make a thorough use of the *vis viva* of the wind, so that when the wind increases one is able to steer against it, and when it decreases one can fly with it, getting beyond the same. One will feel here a similar effect, as already described by Professor Langley in his celebrated treatise entitled "The Internal Work of the Wind." It is no easy step from the theoretical conviction to the practical execution. The dexterity required to allow one'sself to be borne by the wind alone, by describing well-directed circles, is only understood by those who are well acquainted with the difficulties one encounters with the wind. And yet all that may be acquired by practice. When the time comes that athletic associations emulate each other, such results will not be long in following.

Moreover, experimenters will proceed from simple floating and sailing, which in any case form the foundation for practical flight, by degrees to flying with movable implements. As one is enabled to balance himself for some time in the air, the foundations for more extended dynamic effects are easily and safely attained. The different projects may be easily tried by adding the motor work to the simple sailing flight taken as a basis. In this manner one will soon find out the best methods; for practical experience in the air is far better than figuring on paper.

The only thing which may cause difficulties is the procuring of a suitable place for practising.

Just as the starting from the earth is rather difficult for larger birds, the human body, being still heavier, meets with peculiar difficulties at the first flight upward. The larger birds take a running start against the wind or throw themselves into the air from elevated points, in order to obtain free use of their pinions. As soon, however, as they float in the air, their flight, which was begun under special difficulties, is easily continued. The case is similar in human flight. The principal difficulty is the launching into the air, and that will always necessitate special preparations. A man will also have to take a running start against the wind with his flying apparatus, but on a horizontal surface even that will not be sufficient to free himself from the earth. But, on taking a running start from a correspondingly inclined surface, it is easy to begin one's flight even if there is no wind.

According to the example of birds, man will have to start against the wind; but as an inclined surface is necessary for this he needs a hill having the shape of a flat cone, from the top of which he may take starts against the wind in any direction.

Such a place is absolutely necessary, if one wishes to make flying experiments in a convenient way without being dependent on the direction of the wind.

For this purpose I have had an artificial hill, 15 metres high, erected near my house in Gross Lichterfelde, near Berlin, and so have been enabled to make numerous experiments. The drawings show this hill, or part of the same, from the outside. Fig. 9 represents a section of it, showing the cavity in the top intended for keeping the apparatus. At the same time the line of flight taken in calm weather is shown by dotted lines.

If a place for this sport is procured where young persons wishing to indulge in flight can disport themselves in the air, they will then have a chance to make instructive and interesting sailing flights, and I should advise having the hill twice as high, and to form it according to Fig. 10, so that one can commence the flights from a height of 30 metres. The cavity inside should be large enough to hold several complete machines.

Plate IV.

Fig. 7.

Fig. 8.

Intentionally blank as was the original edition.

From such a hill one can take flight of 200 metres distance, and the floating through the air on such long distances affords indescribable pleasure. Added to which this highly exciting exercise is not dangerous, as one can effect a safe landing at any time.

Such a place in which young men can practise sailing flights and can at times make motor experiments with the wings would prove to be of great interest, both to those participating and to the public in general.

And when, from time to time, competitive flights were arranged, we should soon have a national amusement in this as in other sports which we have already. One can see even now that the pleasure and interest of the public in such races, when the gymnasts skilled in flights, shoot through the air, would be greater and more intense than, for instance, in horse or boat racing. The air is the freest element; it admits of the most unfettered movement, and the motion through it affords the greatest delight not only to the person flying, but also to those looking on. It is with astonishment and admiration that we follow the air gymnast swinging himself from trapeze to trapeze; but what are these tiny springs as compared to the powerful bound which the sailer in the air is able to take from the top of the hill, and which carries him over the ground for hundreds of yards?

If the atmosphere is undisturbed, the experimenter sails with uniform speed; as soon, however, as even a slight breeze springs up, the course of the flight becomes irregular, as indicated in Fig. 10. The apparatus inclines now to the right, now to the left.

The person flying ascends from the usual line of flight, and, borne by the wind, suddenly remains floating at a point high up in the air; the on-lookers hold their breath; all at once cheers are heard, the sailer proceeds and glides amid the joyful exclamations of the multitude in a graceful curve back again to the earth.

Can any sport be more exciting than flying? Strength and adroitness, courage and decision, can nowhere gain such tri-

umphs as in these gigantic bounds into the air, when the gymnast safely steers his soaring machine house-high over the heads
of the spectators.

That the danger here is easily avoided when one practises in
a reasonable way, I have sufficiently proved, as I myself have
made thousands of experiments within the last five years, and
have had no accidents whatever, a few scratches excepted.

But all this is only a means to the end ; our aim remains — the
developing of human flight to as high a standard as possible.
If we can succeed in enticing to the hill the young men who
to-day make use of the bicycle and the boat to strengthen their
nerves and muscle, so that, borne by their wings, they may
glide through the air, we shall then have directed the development of human flight into a course which leads towards perfection.

COPY OF LETTERS-PATENT

GRANTED TO

OTTO LILIENTHAL, OF BERLIN, GERMANY, FOR FLYING MACHINE.

SPECIFICATION forming part of Letters-Patent — No. 544816, dated
August 20, 1895.

Application filed February 28, 1894. *Serial No.* 501880. (*No Model.*)

To all whom it may concern :

Be it known that I, OTTO LILIENTHAL, manufacturer, a subject of the
German Emperor, and a resident of Berlin, German Empire, have invented
certain new and useful Improvements in Flying Machines, of which the following is a specification.

This invention relates to flying machines which resemble in their construction the structure of birds' wings. The object of these flying machines is to
imitate the soaring of birds as well as their ordinary flight, which is effected
by the flapping of the wings. The improved machine comprises two wings,
which, after the manner of birds' wings, are slightly vaulted upward. These
wings are fixed by two rods laid crosswise one upon the other and firmly connected together, which rods form a carrying-frame, or part of a carrying-
frame, to which the person intending to fly may hold, so as to be suspended
between the two wings.

Plate V.

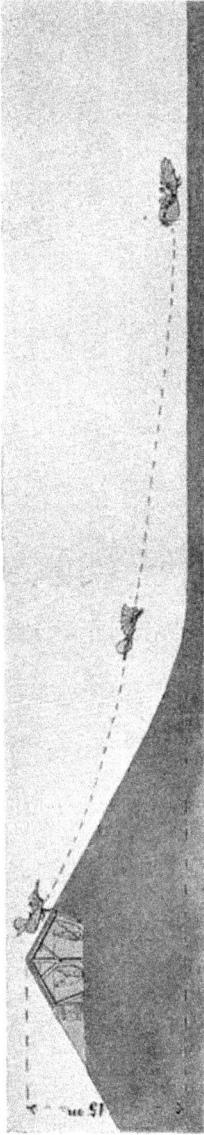

Fig. 9.

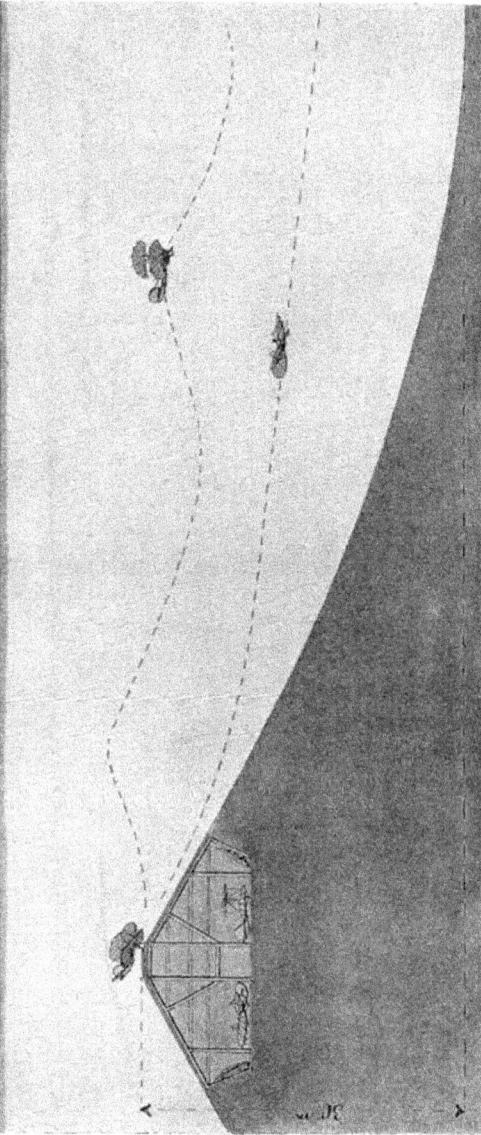

Fig. 10.

Intentionally blank as was the original edition.

In the accompanying drawings the flying machine, constructed according to the present invention, is represented in Figures 1 to 5.

Fig. 1 shows a view from above of this flying machine. Figs. 2, 3, and 4 are sections on the lines A B, C D, and E F of Fig. 1. Fig. 5 shows the flying machine when folded up.

In carrying this invention into practice, two wooden rods a, forming an acute-angled cross, are arranged to carry at their upper ends b pockets d, produced by two small wooden plates. In these pockets are pivoted the wooden ribs e of the wings. A string f, connecting the points of the ribs, and a wire g, fastened to the first rib of the wing and hooked to the hoop h, stretch these ribs in the horizontal direction. The tension downward is given to the ribs by wires i, which extend from the points k of the ribs to the lower ends c of the crossed rods a. Cushions l are fixed between the crossed rods a. The said hoop h is nailed, glued, or otherwise secured in the pockets d. With this hoop are firmly connected the rods m, to which are attached in front the wooden bar n, with the rods o o, and at the rear two diverging rods p. On the latter is pivoted the tail q in such a manner that it can freely turn upward, but finds downward a point of support on the fixed rudder r. This mode of attaching the tail has the advantage that the tail will have no carrying action when the machine is employed like an ordinary parachute, thereby preventing the machine from turning over forward. The rudder r, which serves for automatically keeping the machine in the wind's eye, is likewise detachably fastened to the rods m and the hoop h. The surfaces of the machine over which fabric is stretched are shaded in the right-hand half of Fig. 1.

For using this flying machine, the person inserts his fore-arms between the cushions l, fixed to the crossed wooden rods a, Fig. 3, and takes hold of the bar n with the hands, so that, without changing the upright position of his body, he can carry and properly adjust the machine in a very convenient manner during his run before the flight, while during the flight he can balance and steer the machine, in which he is suspended, by a suitable movement of his body, so as to displace its centre of gravity. In this manner he can imitate the so-called " soaring " of birds, in which the movement takes place merely by a change in the position of the wings with regard to the direction of the wind, there being no rudder movement proper of the wings. As under these circumstances the legs are always freely suspended downward, the landing can safely be effected by putting the feet on the ground.

The folding up of the machine is effected by disengaging the front tension-wires g from the hoop h, turning the ribs about their centre in the pockets d to the rear, and hooking the tension-wires g into the eyes on the rods m. The apparatus then constitutes a compact whole.

Having now particularly described and ascertained the nature of my said invention, and in what manner the same is to be performed, I declare that what I claim, and desire to secure by Letters-Patent of the United States of America, is —

1. In a flying machine, the combination of two crossed carrying rods a, two wings vaulted upward, and strings or wires i extending from the ends of the carrying rods toward the peripheries of the wings, substantially as set forth.

2. In a flying machine, the combination of two crossed carrying rods a, two wings vaulted upward, strings or wires i connecting the two carrying rods with the wings, and a vertical fixed rudder, substantially as set forth.

3. In a flying machine, the combination of a crossed frame, two wings connected therewith, strings or wires i, a vertical fixed rudder r and a horizontal tail q, adapted to turn upward automatically, substantially as set forth.

4. In a flying machine, the combination with a supporting frame, of a

wing adapted to be folded together and having its ribs diverging from a common support, and suitably hinged thereto a string connecting the outer points of the ribs, and continuous fabric attached to a series of ribs, substantially as set forth.

5. In a flying machine, the combination with a supporting frame, comprising a hoop, of a wing having its ribs diverging from a common support, a string connecting the outer points of the ribs, a wire, as g, fastened to the first rib of the wing and attached to the hoop and fabric stretched over the ribs and such wire, substantially as set forth.

6. In a flying machine, the combination with a supporting frame, of a wing having its ribs diverging from a common support, fabric stretched over the ribs and wires, as i, extending from the ribs downward to the supporting frame for the purpose of adjusting thereby the tension of the ribs, substantially as set forth.

7. In a flying machine, the combination with a frame, comprising a hoop and crossed bars, connected therewith, of wings supported by said frame, substantially as set forth.

8. In a flying machine, a supporting frame for the wings comprising a hoop h, rods extending from it for supporting the operator and a tail and a rudder, and pockets as d for receiving the ends of the ribs of the wings, substantially as set forth.

9. In a flying machine, the combination with a supporting frame, of wings with suitable ribs connected therewith, front tension wires g, and pockets d for receiving the inner ends of the ribs, the ribs being made capable of turning around their centres in such pockets for the purpose of folding up such wings, substantially as set forth.

10. In a flying machine, the combination with a supporting frame, of wings, a fixed rudder and a pivoted tail adjusted to come to rest upon the rudder when swinging downward, substantially as set forth.

Signed at Berlin this 1st day of February, 1894.

OTTO LILIENTHAL.

Witnesses:

HERMAN MULLER,
REINHOLD WEIDNER.

MR. LILIENTHAL DESIRES TO HAVE IT ANNOUNCED THAT HIS AMERICAN PATENT RIGHTS ARE FOR SALE, AND THAT UPON APPLICATION HE WILL BE PLEASED TO GIVE FURTHER INFORMATION CONCERNING THEM. HIS ADDRESS IS OTTO LILIENTHAL, 113 KÖPNICKER-STR., — BERLIN, SO., — GERMANY. — ED.

Plate **VI.**

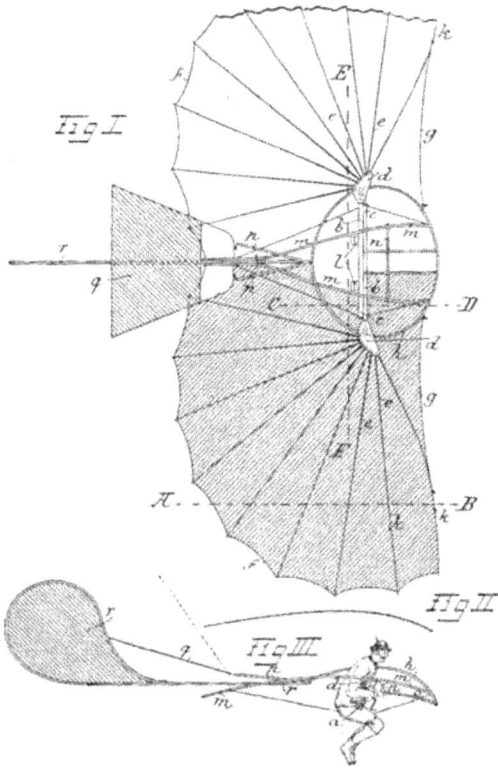

Fig.I.

Fig.II.

Fig.III.

Fig.4.

Fig.5.

Intentionally blank as was the original edition.

WHEELING AND FLYING.

By the Editor.

THE slow development of the flying machine in its early stages finds its analogue in that of the bicycle. The admirable wheel of to-day is the product of more than eighty years of careful thought and experiment.

The machine has been improved very gradually; most of the modifications have been slight; yet some of the stages have been marked with great distinctness.

The twelve machines here shown in the drawings give a rough outline of the progress made. First, we have the wheel of 1816 (Fig. 1), propelled by striking the feet against the ground. This machine represents the parent form, involving the great principle of two wheels balanced by the act of turning the forward wheel on a pivot. It was used principally for the purposes of sport, and it is easily seen that it was at its best on down grades.

Looking backward, it seems strange to us that a device so simple as a pair of foot cranks attached to the front axle was not soon adopted, yet the discovery of such simple things sometimes takes years of hard thinking. Columbus was doubtless surprised when the superficial people of his day told him on his return that any sailor might have discovered the distant land, "all one had to do was to sail west." His alleged reply, illustrated by the balancing of the egg, was most appropriate. The inventor of the sewing machine informed the world that all through the centuries the sewing needle had been threaded at the wrong end; no one knows how long it took him to think that out. We do know, however, in the case of the wheel, that it took many years to think of putting foot cranks on the front axle.

Mr. Porter says [1] that in 1821 Gompertz invented the " Hobby Horse" shown in Fig. 2, and that in 1840 McMillan made a rear-driving machine as shown in Fig. 3.

He quotes M. de Saunier as saying that the honors of first applying foot cranks to the front axle seem to be evenly divided between Michaux and Lallement, who probably worked independently of each other, the former applying the cranks in 1855, the latter in 1863.

Lallement's machine of 1866 is shown in Fig. 4. This was the machine which immediately preceded the velocipede excitement of the late sixties.

Fig. 5 shows the improvement made from 1866 to 1869.

Mr. Porter says, " In 1871 W. H. J. Grant proposed the use of rubber pedals, . . . and he also vulcanized rubber tires into crescent-shaped metal rims."

" In 1873 there was produced by Starley, 'the Father of the Bicycle,' about the first machine (Fig. 6) embodying most of the features which are found in the modern Ordinary."

The Ordinary was greatly improved in the ten or twelve succeeding years (see Fig. 7), and long distance riding became common, yet the dangers attending the use of the high machine gradually led to the designing of lower wheels, of which types are shown in Figs. 8, 9, 10, and 11.

Later came the safety with cushion tires, which was followed, at last, by the pneumatic Safety of to-day (Fig. 12). This is a mere outline; the intermediate machines were many.

It is not uncommon for the cyclist, in the first flush of enthusiasm which quickly follows the unpleasantness of taming the steel steed, to remark, " Wheeling is just like flying ! " This is true in more ways than one. Let us note the points of resemblance. Both modes of travel are riding upon the air, though in one case a small quantity of air is carried in a bag and in the other the air is unbagged. There are many who

[1] See *Wheels and Wheeling*, by Luther H. Porter. Published by The Wheelman Co., 12 Pearl st., Boston. 387 pp. 75 cents. The editor of The Annual is indebted to the author of the above interesting and valuable work for the principal facts concerning bicycles mentioned in this article. The cuts 1 to 11 are taken from Mr. Porter's book, he having kindly consented to their reproduction.

Plate VII.

Fig. 1. CELERIPEDE. 1816.

Fig. 2. HOBBY-HORSE. 1821.

Fig. 3. McCALL'S COPY OF McMILLAN'S REAR-DRIVER. 1840.

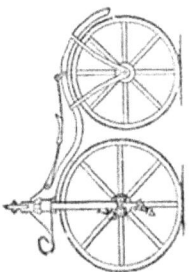

Fig. 4. LALLEMENT'S VELOCIPEDE. 1866.

Fig. 5. AMERICAN VELOCIPEDE. 1869.

Fig. 6. ARIEL BICYCLE. 1873.

Fig. 7. "ORDINARY" BICYCLE. 1886.

Fig. 8. BICYCLETTE. 1880.

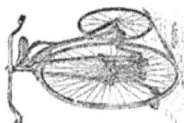

Fig. 9. KANGAROO SAFETY. 1883.

Fig. 10. MARVEL SAFETY. 1884.

Fig. 11. ORIGINAL ROVER SAFETY. 1884.

Fig. 12. PNEUMATIC SAFETY. 1896.

THE DEVELOPMENT OF THE WHEEL.

Intentionally blank as was the original edition.

believe that in order to travel upon air it is not necessary to put the air in a bag; they not only believe this but they know it has been done. Lilienthal has done it many times, and the Lilienthal machine is to flying, what the wheel of 1816 was to pneumatic wheeling. The Lilienthal machine seems likely to lead to important things, yet there are men who say of the inventor: "He cannot fly up, he can only fly down, he is a parachutist, a flying squirrel, he has not solved the great problem." True, he has not solved it, but he has given a partial solution which will place his name on the roll of the immortals.

It is not unlikely that men regarded the wheel of 1816 as some now regard the Lilienthal soarer. They probably said, "This machine will do for coasting down hill, but that is not practical travelling. You cannot climb hills with the thing; it is not of much importance anyhow." But after a while, one day a man who thought put cranks on that machine!

Lilienthal flies not only down, but also up. His course as a whole is downward, but when under favoring winds he gets energy from beneath he rises. The only reason that his course as a whole is not upward is that he has not yet completed his apparatus for giving constant energy.

That will take time, and if the world is to make rapid progress in manflight it must have a much greater confidence in the value and importance of the Lilienthal soarer than it had in the wonderful balancing wheel of 1816. It was a balancing wheel, and the great art of balancing began with it. To learn to wheel one must learn to balance; to learn to fly one must learn to balance. Why not begin now, instead of imitating the human race of the first half of the century which took so many years to get its feet off the ground?

NATURAL AND ARTIFICIAL FLIGHT.

By Hiram S. Maxim.

NOTE. — This article is made up of extracts from an unpublished work and contains the results of Mr. Maxim's latest thought. The author proposes soon to publish the work in full. The whole forms a thesis which was recently sent to the Secretary of the Smithsonian Institution in competition for the Hodgkins prizes. The committee in charge of the Hodgkins Fund awarded to Mr. Maxim honorable mention and a medal for the thesis.

It is speaking quite within bounds to say that this is the most important work which has yet come from this author's pen. — *Ed.*

I.

INTRODUCTORY.

At the time I commenced my experiments in aeronautics it was not generally believed that it would ever be possible to make a large machine heavier than the air that would lift itself from the earth by dynamic energy generated by the machine itself. It is true that a great number of experiments had been made with balloons, but these are in no sense true flying machines. Every one who attempted a solution of the question by machines heavier than the air, was looked upon in very much the same light as the man is now who attempts to construct a perpetual motion machine. Up to within a few years, nearly all experiments in aerial navigation by flying machines have been made by men not versed in science, and who for the most part have been ignorant of the most rudimentary laws of dynamics. It is only quite recently that scientific engineers have

Plate VIII.

MR. MAXIM HOLDING ONE OF HIS ENGINES FOR THE PHOTOGRAPHER.

Intentionally blank as was the original edition.

taken up the question and removed it from the hands of charla-
tans and mountebanks.   A few years ago many engineers would
not have dared to face the ridicule which they would be liable
to receive if they had asserted that it would be possible to make
a machine that would lift itself by mechanical means into the
air.   However, thanks to the admirable work of Professor
Langley, Professor Thurston, Mr. Chanute and others, one may
now express his opinion freely on this subject and speculate as
to the possibilities of making flying machines, without being
relegated to the realm of cranks and fanatics.

During the last five years I have had occasion to write a large
number of articles for the public press on this subject, and I
have always attempted, as far as it is in my power, to discuss
the subject in such a manner as to be easily understood by the
unscientific, and I believe that my efforts have done something
in the direction of popularizing the idea that it is possible to
construct practical flying machines.

In preparing my present work, I have aimed as far as
possible to discuss the question in plain and simple language,
and to abstain from the use of any formulæ which may not
be understood by every one.   It has been my experience that
if a work abounds in formulæ and tables, even only a few of
the scientific will take the trouble to read or understand it.
I have therefore confined myself to a plain statement of the
actual facts, describing the character of my observations and
experiments, and giving the results of the same.   All experiments made by others in the same direction have been on a
very small scale, and, as a rule, the apparatus employed has
been made to travel around a circle, the size of which has not
been great enough to prevent the apparatus continually en-
countering air which had been influenced in some way by the
previous revolution.

The first experiments which I conducted were with an apparatus which travelled around a circle 200 feet in circumference,
and by mounting some delicate anemometers directly under
the path of the apparatus I ascertained that after it had been
travelling at a high velocity for a few seconds, there was a well-

defined air current blowing downward around the whole circle, so that my planes in passing forward must have been influenced and their lifting effect reduced to some extent by this downward current. My late experiments are the first which have ever been made with an apparatus on a large scale moving in a straight line. In discussing the question of aerial flight with Professor Langley before my large experiments had been made, the Professor suggested that there might be some unknown factor relating to size only which might defeat my experiments, and that none of our experiments had at that time been on a sufficiently large scale to demonstrate what the lifting effect of very large planes would be. A flying machine to be of any value must of necessity be large enough to carry at least one man, and the larger the machine the smaller the factor of the man's weight. Moreover, it is possible to make engines of say from 200 to 400 horse-power, lighter per unit of power than very small engines of from one to two horse-power. On the other hand, it is not advisable to construct a machine on too large a scale, because as the machine becomes larger the relative strength of the material becomes less. In first designing my large machine I intended that it should weigh about 5,000 pounds without men, water, or fuel, that the screw thrust should be 1,500 pounds, and that the total area of the planes should be 5,000 square feet. I expected to lift this machine and drive it through the air at a velocity of 35 miles an hour with an expenditure of about 250 horse-power. However, upon completing the machine I found that many parts were too weak, and these had to be supplanted by thicker and stronger material. This increased the weight of the machine about 2,000 pounds. Upon trying my engines I found that if required they would develop 360 horse-power, and that a screw thrust of over 2,000 pounds could be easily attained, but as an offset against this, the amount of power required for driving the machine through the air was a good deal more than I had anticipated.

NOTE.— For Mr. Maxim's description of this machine see "Century Magazine," N.Y., January, 1895.

II.

NATURAL FLIGHT.

During the last 50 years a great deal has been said and written in regard to the flight of birds. Perhaps no other natural phenomenon has excited so much interest and has been so little understood. Learned treatises have been written to prove that a bird is able to develop from 10 to 100 times as much power for its weight as other animals, while other equally learned treatises have shown most conclusively that no greater amount of energy is exerted by a bird in flying than by land animals in running or jumping.

There is no question but what a bird has a higher physical development, as far as the generation of power is concerned, than any other animal we know of. Nevertheless, I think that every one who has made a study of the question will agree that some animals, such as rabbits, exert quite as much power in running in proportion to their weight as a sea-gull or an eagle exerts in flying.

The amount of power which a land animal has to exert is always a fixed and definite quantity. If an animal weighing 100 pounds has to ascend a hill 100 feet high, it always means the development of 10,000 foot-pounds. With a bird, however, there is no such thing as a fixed quantity, because the medium in which the bird is moving is never stationary. If a bird weighing 100 pounds should raise itself into the air 100 feet during a perfect calm, the amount of energy developed would be 10,000 foot-pounds plus the slip of the wings. But, as a matter of fact, the air in which a bird flies is never stationary, as I propose to show; it is always moving either up or down, and soaring birds, by a very delicate sense of feeling, always take advantage of a rising column of air. If a bird finds itself in a column of air which is descending, it is necessary for it to work its wings very rapidly in order to prevent a descent to the earth.

I have often observed the flight of hawks and eagles. They

seem to glide through the air with hardly any movement of
their wings. Sometimes, however, they stop and hold themselves in a stationary position directly over a certain spot, carefully watching something on the earth immediately below. In
such cases they often work their wings with great rapidity,
evidently expending an enormous amount of energy. When,
however, they cease to hover and commence to move again
through the air, they appear to keep themselves at the same
height with an almost imperceptible expenditure of force.

Many unscientific observers of the flight of birds have im-
agined that a wind or a *horizontal* movement of the air is all
that is necessary in order to sustain the weight of a bird in the
air after the manner of a kite. If, however, the wind, which is
only air in motion, should be blowing everywhere at exactly
the same speed and in the same direction (horizontally), it
would offer no more sustaining power to a bird than a dead
calm, because there is nothing to prevent the body of the bird
being blown along with the air, and whenever it had attained
the same velocity as the air, no possible arrangement of the
wings would prevent it from falling to the earth.

The wind, however, seldom or never blows in a horizontal
direction. Some experimenters have lately asserted that if it
were possible for us to ascend far enough, we should find the
temperature constantly falling until at about 20 or 25 miles
above the earth's surface the absolute zero might be reached.
Now, as the air near the earth never falls in temperature to
anything like the absolute zero, it follows that there is a constant change going on, the relatively warm air near the surface
of the earth always ascending, and, in some cases, doing sufficient work in expanding to render a portion of the water it
contains visible, forming clouds, rain, or snow, while the very
cold air is constantly descending to take the place of the rising
column of warm air.

On one occasion while crossing the Atlantic in fine weather,
I noticed, some miles directly ahead of the ship, a long line of
glassy water. Small waves indicated that the wind was blowing
in the exact direction in which the ship was moving, and I

observed as we approached the glassy line that the waves became
smaller and smaller until they completely disappeared in a
mirror-like surface which was about 300 or 400 feet wide and
extended both to the port and starboard in approximately a
straight line as far as the eye could reach. After passing the
centre of this zone, I noticed that small waves began to show
themselves, but in the exact opposite direction to those through
which we had already passed. I observed that these waves
became larger and larger for nearly an hour. Then they began to get gradually smaller, when I observed another glassy
line directly ahead of the ship. As we approached it the waves
completely disappeared, but after passing through it I noticed
that the wind was blowing in the opposite direction and that
the waves increased in size exactly in the same manner that
they had diminished on the opposite side of the glassy zone.

This would seem to indicate that directly over the centre of
the first glassy zone, the air was meeting from both sides and
ascending, and that at the other glassy zone the air was descending in practically a straight line to the surface of the
water where it spread out and set up a light wind in both
directions.

I spent the winter of 1890–91 on the Riviera, between
Hyères les Palmiers and Monte Carlo. The weather for the
most part was very fine, and I often had opportunities of observing the peculiar phenomena which I had already noticed in
the Atlantic, only on a much smaller scale. Whereas, in the
Atlantic, the glassy zones were from 5 to 20 miles apart, I often
found them not more than 500 feet apart in the bays of the
Mediterranean.

At Nice and Monte Carlo this phenomenon was also very
marked. On one occasion, while making observations from the
highest part of the promontory of Monaco on a perfectly calm
day, I noticed that the whole of the sea presented this peculiar
effect as far as the eye could reach, and that the lines which
marked the descending air were never more than a thousand
feet from those which marked the centre of the ascending column.
At about 3 o'clock in the afternoon, a large black steamer

passed along the coast in a perfectly straight line, and I noticed that its wake was at once marked by a glassy line which indicated the centre of an ascending column. This line remained almost straight for two hours, when finally it became crooked and broken. The heat of the steamer had been sufficient to determine this upward current of air.

In 1893, I spent two weeks in the Mediterranean, going by a slow steamer from Marseilles to Constantinople and returning, and I had many opportunities of observing the peculiar phenomenon which I have before referred to. The steamer passed over thousands of square miles of calm sea, the surface being only disturbed by large batches of small ripples separated from each other by glassy streaks, and I found that in no case was the wind blowing in the same direction on both sides of these streaks, every one of them either indicating the centre of an ascending or a descending column of air.

If we should investigate this phenomenon in what might be called a dead calm, we should probably find that the air was rising straight up over the centres of some of these streaks, and descending in a vertical line over the centres of the others. But, as a matter of fact, there is no such thing as a dead calm. The movement of the air is the resultant of more than one force. The air is not only rising in some places and descending in others, but at the same time the whole mass is moving forward with more or less rapidity from one part of the earth to another. So we might consider that, instead of the air ascending directly from the relatively hot surface of the earth and descending vertically in other places, in reality it is moving on an incline.

Suppose that the local influence which causes the up and down motion of the air should be sufficiently great to cause it to rise at the rate of 2 miles an hour, and that the wind at the same time should be blowing at the rate of 10 miles an hour; the motion of the air would then be the resultant of these two velocities. In other words, it would be blowing up an incline of 1 in 5. Suppose now, that a bird should be able to so adjust its wings that it advanced 5 miles in falling 1 mile through a perfectly calm atmosphere; it would be able to sustain itself in an inclined wind, such as I have described, without any movement at all of its wings. If it was able to adjust its wings in such a manner that it could advance 6 miles by falling through 1 mile of air, it would then be able to rise as relates to the earth while in reality falling as relates to the surrounding air.

In conducting a series of experiments with artillery and small guns in a very large and level field just out of Madrid, I often observed the same phenomena as relates to the wind, that I have already spoken of as having observed at sea, except that the lines marking the centre of an ascending or a descending column of air were not so stationary as they were over the water. It was not an uncommon thing when adjusting the sights of a gun to fire at a target at very long range, making due allowances for the wind, to have the wind change and blow in the opposite direction before the word of command was given to fire. While conducting these experiments, I often noticed the flight of eagles. On one occasion a pair of eagles came into sight on one side of the plain, passed directly over our heads and disappeared on the opposite side. They were apparently always at the same height from the earth and soared completely across the plain without once moving their wings. This phenomenon, I think, can only be accounted for on the hypothesis that they were able to feel out with their wings an ascending column of air, that the centre of this column of air was approximately a straight line running completely across the plain, that they found the ascending column to be more than necessary to sustain their weight in the air, and that whereas, as relates to the earth, they were not falling at all, they were really falling some 2 or 3 miles an hour in the air which supported them.

Again, at Cadiz in Spain, when the wind was blowing in very strongly from the sea, I noticed that the sea-gulls always took advantage of an ascending column of air. As the wind blew in from the sea and rose to pass over the fortifications, the sea-gulls selected a place where they could slide down on the ascending current of air, keeping themselves always approximately in the same place without any apparent exertion. When, however, they left this ascending column, I observed that it was necessary for them to work their wings with great vigor until they again found the proper place to encounter the favorable current.

I have often noticed sea-gulls following a ship. I have observed that they are able to follow the ship without any apparent exertion; they simply balance themselves on an ascending column of air and seem to be quite as much at ease as they would be if they were roosting on a solid support. If, however, they are driven out of this position, I find that they generally have to commence at once to work their passage. If anything is thrown overboard which is too heavy for them to lift, the ship soon leaves them, and in order to catch up with it again, they move their wings very much as other birds do; but when once established in the ascending column of air, they manage to keep up with the ship by doing little or no work. In a head wind we find them directly aft of the ship; if the wind is from the port side, they may always be found on the starboard quarter, and *vice versa.*

Every one who has passed a winter on the northern shores of the Mediterranean must have observed the cold wind which is generally called the *mistral.* One may be out driving, the sun may be shining brightly, and the air be warm and balmy, when, suddenly, without any apparent cause, one finds himself in a cold descending wind. This is the much-dreaded mistral, and if at sea, it would be marked by a glassy line on the surface of the water. On land, however, there is nothing to render its presence visible. I have found that the ascending column of air is always very much warmer than the descending column, and that this action is constantly taking place in a greater or less degree.

From the foregoing deductions I think we may draw the following conclusions:

First, that there is a constant interchange of air taking place, the cold air descending, spreading itself out over the surface of the earth, becoming warm, and ascending in other places.

Second that the centres of the two columns are generally separated from each other by a distance which may be from 500 feet to 20 miles.

Third, that the centres of greatest action are not in spots, but in lines which may be approximately straight but generally abound in many sinuosities.

Fourth, that this action is constantly taking place over both the sea and the land, that the soaring of birds, a phenomenon which has heretofore been so little understood, may be accounted for on the hypothesis that the bird seeks out an ascending column of air, and that, while sustaining itself at the same height in the air without any muscular exertion, it is in reality falling at a considerable speed through the air that surrounds it.

It has been supposed by some scientists that the birds may take advantage of some vibratory or rolling action of the air. I find, however, from careful observation and experiment, that the motion of the wind is comparatively steady, and that the short vibratory or rolling action is always very near to the earth and is produced by the air flowing over the tops of hills, high buildings, or trees. If a kite is flown only a few feet above the ground, it will be found that the current of air is very unsteady. If it is allowed to mount to 500 feet, the unsteadiness nearly all disappears, while if it is further allowed to mount to a height of 1,500 or 2,000 feet, the pull on the cord is almost constant, and, if the kite is well made, it remains practically stationary in the air.

I have often noticed in high winds, that light and fleecy clouds come into view, say, about 2,000 feet above the surface of the earth, and that they pass rapidly and steadily by, preserving their shape completely. This would certainly indicate that there is no rapid local disturbance in the air in their immediate vicinity, but that the whole mass of air in which these clouds are formed is practically travelling in the same direction and at the same velocity. Numerous aeronauts have also testified that, no matter how hard the wind may be blowing, the balloon is always practically in a dead calm, and if a piece of gold-leaf is thrown overboard even in a gale, the gold-leaf and the balloon never part company in a horizontal direction, though they may in a vertical direction.

Birds may be divided into two classes: first, the soaring birds, which practically live upon the wing, and which, by some very delicate sense of touch, are able to feel the exact condition of the air. Many fish which live near the top of the water are greatly distressed by sinking too deeply, while others which live at great depths are almost instantly killed by being raised to the surface. The swim bladder of a fish is in reality a delicate barometer provided with sensitive nerves which enable the fish to feel whether it is sinking or rising in the water. With the surface fish, if the pressure becomes too great, the fish involuntarily exerts itself to rise nearer the surface and so diminish the pressure, and I have no doubt that the air-cells, which are known to be very numerous and to abound throughout the bodies of birds, are so sensitive as to enable soaring birds to know at once whether they are in an ascending or a descending column of air.

The other class of birds consists of those which only employ their wings for the purpose of taking them rapidly from one place to another. Such birds may be considered not to expend their power so economically as the soaring birds. They do not spend a very large portion of their time in the air, but what time they are on the wing they exert an immense amount of power and fly very rapidly, generally in a straight line, taking no advantage of air currents. Partridges, pheasants, wild ducks, geese, and some birds of passage may be taken as types of this kind. This class of birds has relatively small wings, and carries about $2\frac{1}{2}$ times as much weight per square foot of surface as soaring birds do.

III.

ARTIFICIAL FLIGHT. — THE ENGINES.

There is no question but what birds — and, for that matter, all animals — when considered as thermo-dynamic machines, are very perfect motors; they develop the full theoretical amount of energy in the carbon consumed. This we are quite unable to do with any artificial machine, but birds for the most part have to content themselves with food which is not very rich in carbon. It is quite true that a bird may develop from 10 to 15 times as much power from the carbon consumed as may be developed by the best steam-engine, but as an offset against this, a steam-engine is able to consume petroleum, which has at least 20 times as many thermal units per pound as the ordinary food of birds. The movement of a bird's wings, from long years of development, has without doubt attained a great degree of perfection. Birds are able to scull themselves through the air with very little loss of energy. To imitate by mechanical means the exact and delicate motion of their wings would certainly be a very difficult task, and I do not believe that we should attempt it in constructing an artificial flying machine. In Nature it is necessary that an animal should be made all in one piece. It is therefore quite out of the question that any part or parts should revolve. For land animals there is no question but what legs are the most perfect system possible, but in terrestrial locomotion by machinery — not necessarily in one piece — the wheel is found to be much more effective and efficient. The swiftest animal can only travel for a minute of time at half the speed of a locomotive, while the locomotive is able to maintain its much greater speed for many hours at a time. The largest land animals only weigh about 5 tons, while the largest locomotives weigh from 60 to 80 tons. In the sea, the largest animal weighs about 75 tons, while the ordinary Atlantic liner weighs from 4,000 to 14,000 tons. The whale no doubt is able to maintain a high speed for several hours at a time, but the modern steamer is able to maintain a still higher speed for many consecutive days.

As artificial machines for terrestrial and aquatic locomotion have been made immensely stronger and larger than land or water animals, so, in a flying machine, it will be necessary to construct it much heavier and stronger than the largest bird. If one should attempt to propel such a machine with wings, it would be quite as difficult a problem to solve as it would be to make a locomotive that would walk on legs. What is required in a flying machine is something to which a very large amount of power can be directly and continuously applied without any intervening levers or joints, and this we find in the screw propeller.

It was about 20 years ago that I first commenced to think of the question of artificial flight. My first idea was to construct a machine with two large screws on vertical shafts. I proposed to run these screws in reverse directions by the use of a caloric or hot-air engine, but after considering the subject for some time, I came to the conclusion that this class of engine would not do. When the Brayton gas engine first made its appearance, I commenced drawings of a machine, using a modification of the Brayton motor which I designed expressly for the purpose; but even this was found to be too heavy, and it was not until after I abandoned the vertical screw system that it was possible for me to design a machine which in theory ought to fly.

The next machine which I considered was on the kite or aeroplane system. This was also to be driven by an oil engine. Oil engines at that time were not so simple as now, and moreover the system of ignition was very heavy, cumbersome, and uncertain. Since that time, however, gas and oil engines have been very much improved, and the ignition tube, which is almost universally used, has greatly simplified the ignition, so that at the present time I am of the opinion that an oil engine might be designed which would be suitable for the purpose.

IV.

THE ADVANTAGES AND DISADVANTAGES OF VERY NARROW PLANES.

My experiments have demonstrated that relatively narrow aeroplanes lift more per square foot than very wide ones, but as an aeroplane, no matter how narrow it may be, must of necessity have some thickness, it is not advantageous to place them too near together. Suppose that aeroplanes should be made $\frac{1}{4}$ in. thick and be superposed 3 inches apart, that is, at a pitch of 3 inches. One-twelfth part of the whole space through which these planes would have to be driven would be occupied by the planes themselves, and eleven-twelfths would be air space (Fig. 1). If a group of planes thus mounted should be driven through the air at the rate of 36 miles an hour,[1] the air would have to be driven forward at the rate of 3 miles an hour, or else

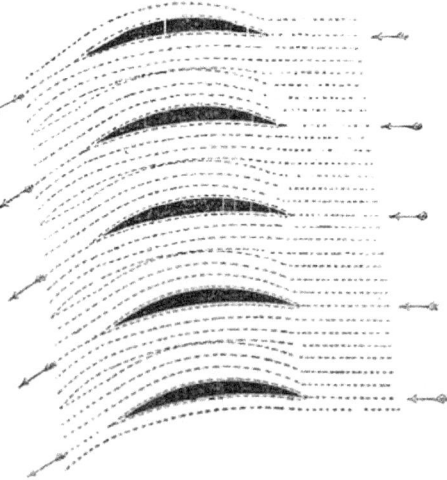

Fig. 1.

it would have to be compressed, or spun out, and pass between the spaces at a speed of 39 miles an hour. As a matter of fact, however, the difference in pressure is so very small, that practically no atmospheric compression takes place. The air, therefore, is driven forward at the rate of 3 miles an hour, and this consumes a great deal of power, in fact, so much that there is a decided disadvantage in using narrow planes thus arranged.

In regard to the curvature of narrow aeroplanes, I have found that if one only desires to lift a large load in proportion to the area, the planes may be made very hollow on the underneath side; but when one considers the lift in terms of screw thrust, I find it advisable that the planes should be as thin as possible and the underneath side nearly flat. I have also found that it is a great advantage to arrange the planes after the manner

[1] The arrows in the accompanying drawings show the direction of the air currents, the experiments having been made with stationary planes and a moving current of air.

shown in Fig. 2.   In this manner, the sum of all the spaces
between the planes is equal to the whole area occupied by the

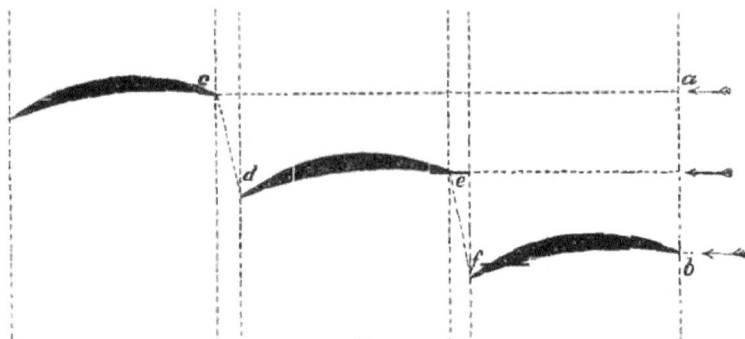

Fig. 2.

planes; consequently, the air neither has to be compressed,
spun out, or driven forward.   I am therefore by this arrangement able to produce a large lifting effect per square foot,
and, at the same time, to keep the screw thrust within reasonable limits.

A large number of experiments with very narrow aeroplanes
have been conducted by Mr. Horatio Phillips at Harrow, in
England.   Fig. 3
shows a cross section
of one of Mr. Phil-
lips' planes.   Mr.
Phillips is of the

Fig. 3.

opinion that the air in striking the top side of the plane is
thrown upward in the manner shown and a partial vacuum is
thereby formed over the central part of the plane, and that
the lifting effect of planes made in this form is therefore
very much greater than with ordinary narrow planes.   I have
experimented with these "sustainers" (as Mr. Phillips calls
them) myself, and I find it is quite true that they lift in some
cases as much as 8 lb. per sq. ft.,[1] but the lifting effect is not

---

[1] In my early experiments I lifted as much as 8 lb. per sq. ft. with aeroplanes which were
only slightly curved, but very thin and sharp.

produced in the exact manner that Mr. Phillips seems to suppose. The air does not glance off in the manner shown. As
the "sustainer" strikes the air, two currents are formed, one
following the exact contour of the top and the other the bottom. These two currents join and are thrown downward as
relates to the "sustainer" at an angle which is the resultant of
the angles at which the two currents meet. (Fig. 4.) These

Fig. 4.

"sustainers" may be made to lift when the front edge is lower
than the rear edge because they encounter still air, and leave it
with a downward motion.

In my experiments with narrow superposed planes, I have
always found that with strips of thin metal made sharp at both
edges and only slightly curved, the lifting effect, when considered in terms of screw thrust, was always greater than with any
arrangement of the wooden aeroplanes used in Phillips' experiments. It would therefore appear that there is no advantage in
the peculiar form of "sustainer" employed by this inventor.

If an aeroplane be made perfectly flat on the bottom side and
convex on the top, as shown in Fig. 5, and be mounted in the
air so that the bottom
side is exactly horizon-
tal, it produces a lifting
effect no matter in which
direction it is run, be-

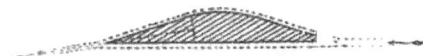

Fig 5.

cause as it advances it encounters stationary air which is divided
into two streams. The top stream being unable to fly off at a
tangent when turning over the top curve, flows down the incline
and joins the current which is flowing over the lower horizontal
surface. The angle at which the combined stream of air leaves
the plane is the resultant of these two angles; consequently, as
the plane finds the air in a stationary condition and leaves it
with a downward motion, the plane itself must be lifted. It is

true that small and narrow aeroplanes may be made to lift considerably more per square foot of surface than very large ones, but they do not offer the same safeguard against a rapid descent to the earth in case of a stoppage or breakdown of the machinery. With a large aeroplane properly adjusted, a rapid and destructive fall to the earth is quite impossible.

In the foregoing experiments with narrow aeroplanes, I employed an apparatus (Fig. 6) which enabled me to mount my planes at any angle in a powerful blast of air, and to weigh the exact lifting effect and also the tendency to drift with the wind. This apparatus also enables me to determine with a great degree of nicety the best form of an atmospheric condenser to employ.

V.

THE EFFICIENCY OF SCREW PROPELLERS. — STEERING, STABILITY, ETC.

Before I commenced my experiments at Baldwyn's Park, I attempted to obtain some information in regard to the action of screw propellers working in the air. I went to Paris and saw the apparatus which the French Government employed for testing the efficiency of screw propellers, but the propellers were so very badly made that the experiments were of no value. Upon consulting an English experimenter who had made a "lifelong study" of the question, he assured me that I should find the screw propeller very inefficient and very wasteful of power. He said that all screw propellers had a powerful fan-blower action, drawing in air at the centre and discharging it with great force at the periphery. I found that no two men were agreed as to the action of screw propellers. All the data or formulæ available were so confusing and contradictory as to be of no value whatsoever. Some experimenters were of the opinion that in computing the thrust of a screw we should only consider the projected area of the blades, and that the thrust would be equal

Plate IX.

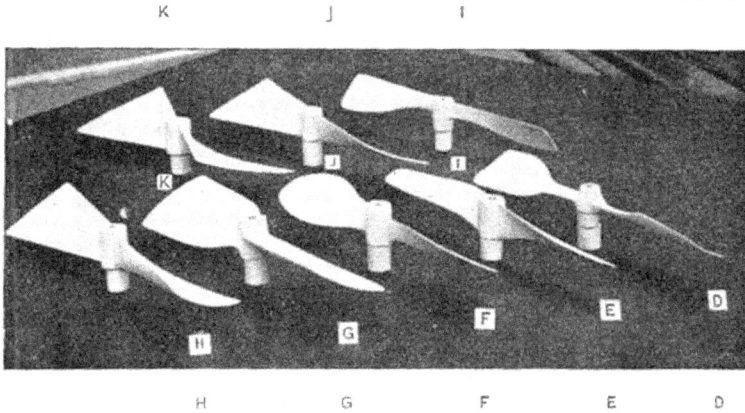

Fig. 13. — A group, showing the various forms of screws which Mr. Maxim has tested. The screw J was found to be the most efficient. A similar screw K, with wider blades, did not do so well. The screw E, although very light and small, did very well. G, a screw made on the French plan, proved the worst screw experimented with. H, the same form as J, except that the blades are much thicker, also did remarkably well.

Fig. 14.

THE THREE PRINCIPAL FORMS OF SCREW EXPERIMENTED WITH.

A. — Plain screw with flat blades.
B. — Screw with slightly curved blades with increasing pitch.
C. — Screw with curved blades, compound increasing pitch.

Fig. 15.

THE FORWARD RUDDER FOR STEERING MR. MAXIM'S MACHINE IN A
VERTICAL DIRECTION.

This plate is especially interesting as showing the construction of the framing. — Ed.

Intentionally blank as was the original edition.

to a wind blowing against a normal plane of equal area at a velocity equal to the slip. Others were of the opinion that the whole screw disk would have to be considered; that is, that the thrust would be equal to a wind blowing against a normal plane equal to the area of the whole disk at the velocity of the slip. The projected area of the two screw blades of my machine is 94 square feet, and the area of the 2 screw disks is 500 square feet. According to the first system of reasoning, therefore, the screw thrust of my large machine, when running at 40 miles an hour with a slip of 18 miles per hour, would have been, according to the well-known formula, $V^2 \times .005 = P$

$$18^2 \times .005 \times 94 = 152.28 \text{ pounds.}$$

If, however, we should have considered the whole screw disk, it would have been —

$$18^2 \times .005 \times 500 = 810 \text{ pounds.}$$

However, when the machine was run over the track at this rate, the thrust was found to be rather more than 2,000 lbs. When the machine was secured to the track and the screws revolved until the pitch in feet multiplied by the turns per minute was equal to 68 miles an hour, it was found that the screw thrust was 2,164 lbs. In this case it was of course all slip, and when the screws had been making a few turns they had established a well-defined air-current, and the power exerted by the engines was simply to maintain this air-current, and it is interesting to note that if we compute the projected area of these blades by the foregoing formula, the thrust would be —

$$68^2 \times .005 \times 94 = 2173.28 \text{ pounds,}$$

which is almost exactly the observed screw thrust. From this, it would appear when the machine is stationary, and all the power is consumed in slip, that only the projected area of the screw blades should be considered. But whenever the machine is allowed to advance, and to encounter new air, the inertia of which has not been disturbed, the efficiency increases in geometrical progression. The exact rate for all speeds I have not yet ascertained. My experiments have, however, shown that with a speed of 40 miles an hour and a screw slip of 18 miles an hour, a well-made screw

propeller is 13.1 times as efficient as early experimenters had
supposed and attempted to prove by elaborate formulæ.

When I first commenced my experiments with a large machine, I did not know exactly what form of boiler, gas generator, or burner I should finally adopt; I did not know the exact
size that it would be necessary to make my engines; I did not
know the size, the pitch, or the diameter of the screws which
would be the most advantageous. Neither did I know the form
of aeroplane which I should finally adopt. It was therefore
necessary for me to make the foundation or platform of my machine of such a character that it would allow me to make the
modifications necessary to arrive at the best results. The platform of the machine is therefore rather larger than is necessary,
and I find if I were to design a completely new machine, that it
would be possible to greatly reduce the weight of the framework, and, what is still more, to greatly reduce the force necessary to drive it through the air.

At the present time, the body of my machine[1] is a large platform, about 8 ft. wide and 40 ft. long. Each side is formed of
very strong trusses of steel tubes, braced in every direction by
strong steel wires. The trusses which give stiffness to this
superstructure are all below the platform. In designing a new
machine, I should make the trusses much deeper and at the
same time very much lighter, and, instead of having them below
the platform on which the boiler is situated, I should have them
constructed in such a manner as to completely enclose the
boiler and the greater part of the machinery. I should make
the cross-section of the framework rectangular, and pointed
at each end. I should cover the outside very carefully with
balloon material, giving it a perfectly smooth and even surface
throughout, so that it might be easily driven through the air.

In regard to the screws, I am at the present time able to
mount screws 17 ft. 10 in. in diameter. I find, however, that my
machine would be much more efficient if the screws were 24
feet in diameter, and I believe with such very large screws, four
blades would be much more efficient than two.

[1]See *A New Flying Machine*, by H. S. Maxim. Century Magazine, N. Y., January,
1895. — *Ed.*

My machine may be steered to the right or to the left by running one of the propellers faster than the other. Very convenient throttle valves have been provided to facilitate this system of steering. An ordinary vertical rudder placed just after the screws may, however, prove more convenient, if not more efficient.

The machine is provided with fore and aft horizontal rudders, both of which are connected with the same windlass. If the forward rudder is placed at an angle considerably greater than that of the main aero-plane, and the rear rud-der placed flat so as not to lift at all (Fig. 7), and the machine run over the track at a high speed, the front wheels will be lifted

Fig. 7. — The forward wheels off the track.

from the steel rails, leaving the rear wheels on the rails. If the rudders are placed in the reverse position so that the front rudder

Fig. 8. — The rear wheels off the track.

is thrown out of action, and the rear rudder lifts to its full extent (Fig. 8), the hind wheels will be lifted from the steel rails, leaving only the forward wheels touching. If both rudders are placed at such an angle that they both lift (Fig. 9), and the ma-chine is run at a very high velocity, all four of the wheels will be lifted from the steel rails. This would seem to show that these rudders are efficient as far as vertical steering is concerned. If the machine should break down in the air it would be

Fig. 9. — All the wheels off the track.

necessary to tilt the rudders in the position shown in Fig. 10, when it would fall to the ground without pitching or diving.

In regard to the stability of the machine, the centre of weight is much below the centre of lifting effect; moreover, the upper wings are set at such an angle that whenever the machine tilts

to the right or to the left, the lifting effect is increased on the lower side and diminished on the higher side (Fig. 11). This simple arrangement makes the machine automatic as far as rolling is concerned. I am

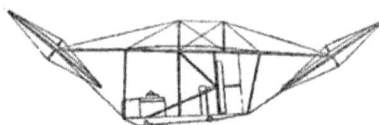

Fig. 10. — Showing the manner of placing the fore and aft rudders in case of a breakage of the machinery.

of the opinion that whenever flying machines come into use it will be necessary to steer them in a vertical direction by means

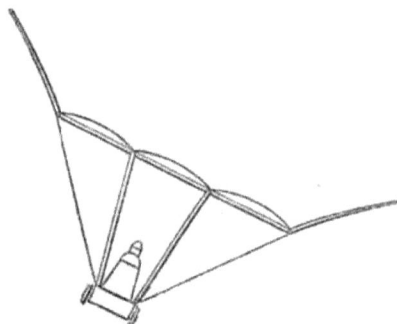

Fig. 11.

of an automatic steering gear controlled by a gyroscope. It will certainly not be more difficult to manœuvre and steer such machines than it is to control completely submerged torpedoes.

When the machine is once perfected, it will not require a railway track to enable it to get the necessary velocity to rise. A short run over a moderately level field will

suffice. As far as landing is concerned, the aerial navigator will touch the ground while moving forward, and the machine will be brought to a state of rest by sliding on the ground for a short distance. In this manner very little shock will result, whereas if the machine is stopped in the air and allowed to fall directly to the earth without advancing, the shock, although not strong enough to be dangerous to life or limb, might be sufficient to disarrange or injure the machinery.

VI.

THE COMPARATIVE VALUE OF DIFFERENT MOTORS.

So far I have only discussed the navigation of the air by the use of propellers driven by a steam engine. The engines that I employ are what are known as compound engines, that is, they have a large and a small cylinder. Steam at a very high pressure enters the high pressure cylinder, expands and escapes at a lower pressure into a larger cylinder where it again expands and does more work. A compound engine is more economical in steam than a simple engine, and therefore requires a smaller boiler to develop the same horse-power, so that when we consider the weight of water and fuel for a given time, together with the weight of the boiler and the engine, the complete motor with a compound engine is lighter than a simple engine. However, if only the weight of the engine is to be considered, then the simple engine will develop more power per unit of weight than the compound engine. For instance, if instead of allowing the steam to enter the small cylinder, and the exhaust from this cylinder to enter the large or low-pressure cylinder, which necessitates that the high-pressure piston has to work against a back-pressure equal to the full pressure in the low-pressure cylinder, I should connect both cylinders direct with the live steam and allow both to discharge their exhaust directly into the air. I should then have a pair of simple engines, and instead of developing 363 horse-power, they would develop fully 500 horse-power, or nearly 1 horse-power for every pound of their weight. I mention this fact to show that the engines are exceedingly light, and that when compared with simple engines their power should be computed on the same basis. It will therefore be seen that if we do not take into consideration the steam supply or the amount of fuel and water necessary, the simple steam engine is an exceedingly light motor.

But as before stated, great improvements have recently been made in oil engines. I have thought much on this subject, and am of the opinion that if one had an unlimited supply of money,

a series of experiments could be very profitably conducted with
a view of adapting the oil engine for use on flying machines. If
we use a steam engine it is necessary to have a boiler, and at
the best a boiler is rather a large and heavy object to drive
through the air. If we use an oil engine no boiler is necessary
and the amount of heat carried over in the cooling water will
only be one-seventh part of what is carried over in the exhaust
from a steam engine of the same power. Therefore the condenser need only be one-seventh part of the size, and consequently could be made lighter with the tubes placed at a greater
distance apart, and thus reduce the amount of power necessary
to drive the machine through the air. Moreover, the supply of
water necessary will be greatly reduced and a cheaper and
heavier oil may be employed which is not so liable to take fire
in case of an accident. It is, then, only a question as to whether
an oil engine can be made so light as to keep its weight within
that of a steam motor; that is, an oil-engine in order to be
available for the purpose must be as light, including its water
supply, as a complete steam motor which includes not only the
engine, but also the boiler, the feed-pumps, the water supply,
the burner, the gas generator, and six-sevenths of the condenser.
It requires a very perfect steam-engine and boiler, not using a
vacuum, to develop a horse-power with a consumption of $1\frac{1}{2}$
pounds of petroleum per hour; but there are many oil engines
which develop a horse-power with rather less than one pound
of oil per hour. It will therefore be seen that as far as fuel is
concerned the oil engine has a decided advantage over the more
complicated steam motor. Moreover, with an oil engine the
cooling water is not under pressure, so that the waste of water
would be much less than with a steam engine, where the pressure is so high as to cause a considerable amount of waste
through joints, valves, and numerous stuffing boxes.

The great advances that have been made of late years in
electrical science and engineering have led many to believe that
almost any knotty scientific question could be solved by the
employment of electrical agencies, and a great deal has been

written and said in regard to navigating the air by flying machines driven by electric motors.

Before I commenced my experiments I made inquiries of all the prominent electrical engineering establishments where there was any likelihood of obtaining light and efficient electric motors, and I found that it was impossible to obtain one that would develop a horse-power for any considerable time that would weigh less than 150 lbs. Since that time, notwithstanding that a great deal has appeared in the public prints about the efficiency and lightness of electric motors, I am unable to learn of any concern that is ready to furnish a complete motor, including a primary or secondary battery which would supply the necessary current for two hours at a time, at a weight of less than 150 lbs. per horse-power, and as far as I have been able to ascertain from what I have myself seen, I cannot learn that there are any motors in practical use which do not weigh, including their storage batteries, at least 300 lbs. per horse-power. The last electric motor which I examined was in a boat; it was driven by a primary battery which weighed over 1,000 lbs. to the horse-power. From this I am of the opinion that we can not at present look to electricity with any hope of finding a motor which is suitable for the purpose of aerial navigation.

VII.

CONCLUSION.

My large machine, which was injured in my late experiments, has now been repaired and improved, and is quite ready to be used in any other experiments which I may wish to make on the limited area which I now have at my disposal. The railway track on which my experiments have been made is 1,800 feet long and the land on all sides is thickly studded with large trees. When making experiments about 500 feet of the track is used in getting up the necessary speed and 300 feet is utilized in bringing the machine again to a state of rest. My clear run is therefore limited to 1,000 feet, and the time which the machine takes to pass over this length of rail is at the most only a few seconds. It will therefore be seen that it is not an easy matter to conduct experiments in a satisfactory manner. In addition to these experiments with a large machine, I am also conducting a series of experiments in a blast of air issuing from a trunk 3 feet square. The air is set in motion by the action of screw propellers driven by a steam engine of 60 horse-power, and I am able to obtain any atmospheric velocity that I require, from 5 to 90 miles an hour. This apparatus is shown in Fig. 6, and is constructed in such a manner that it enables me to mount in this current of air any object that I wish to experiment with. For instance, a bar of wood 3 inches square is mounted in the blast of air so that one of its sides forms a normal plane perpendicular to the direction of the blast. The engine is then run until the air is passing through the trunk at a velocity of 50 miles an hour. The tendency of this bar of wood to travel in the direction of the air may then be accurately determined, and this is considered as unity. A cylinder exactly 3 inches in diameter may then be mounted and tested in the same manner. The cylinder will of course have less tendency to travel with the air than the square bar of wood, and whatever this tendency is, will be the coefficient of a cylinder. I have provided oval, elliptical, and various other shaped objects to be experimented with, and when the experiments are finished I shall know the exact coefficient of all shapes that it may be practical to use in the framework of a flying machine, and also what effect is produced by placing two or more bodies in close proximity to each other.

In addition to these experiments, I am also able with the same air blast to ascertain the efficiency of various forms of aeroplanes, superposed or otherwise, and placed at all angles, the apparatus being provided with a scale beam which not only enables me to measure the drift, but also to accurately weigh the lifting effect. The aeroplane, or grouping of aeroplanes, in

Plate X.

Fig. 6.

AIR-BLAST APPARATUS FOR MEASURING THE LIFT AND DRIFT OF
AEROPLANES AND AEROCURVES.

Fig. 12.

THE RESULT OF AN ACCIDENT TO MR. MAXIM'S MACHINE.

This shows one of the wheels which pulled upward on the upper rail. The lifting power of the
machine caused the axle to yield as here shown.

Intentionally blank as was the original edition.

which the drift will go the greatest number of times into the lift will be considered the most satisfactory for the purpose.

Experiments are also being made in the same air blast with a view of ascertaining the condensing and lifting power of various forms of tubes, steam in the condition of exhaust being passed through the tubes while the air is driven between them at any velocity required. The experiments are being made with pure steam and also with steam contaminated with oil, with a view of ascertaining to what extent the efficiency of the condenser is reduced by a film of oil such as may be expected from exhaust steam. These experiments will enable me to ascertain very exactly the weight and the efficiency of atmospheric condensers, the amount that their tubes may be made to lift at various speeds and atmospheric conditions, and will also enable me to select the form which I find most suitable for the purpose.

In navigating a boat, it is only necessary that one should be able to turn it to the right or to the left (port or starboard), but with a flying machine it is not only necessary to steer it to the right or left (horizontally), but also in a vertical direction to prevent it from rearing up forward or pitching, and this, if it is accomplished by hand, will require the constant vigilance of a man at the wheel who can make observations, think, and act instantly. In order to prevent a too rapid up and down deviation of the machine I have constructed it of great length, so that the man at the helm will have more time to think and act. As before stated, however, I am of the opinion that the steering in a vertical direction should be automatically controlled by a gyroscope, and I have made an apparatus which consists of a steam piston acting directly upon the fore and aft rudders, the steam valve being controlled by a gyroscope. As the rudders are moved by the steam, their movement shuts the steam off in exactly the same manner that the moving of a rudder shuts off the steam in the well-known steam-steering apparatus now universally in use on all large steamers.

Now that it is definitely known that it is possible to construct a large machine which is light enough and at the same time powerful enough to raise its own weight and that of its engineers into the air, the next question which presents itself for solution is to ascertain how to steer and control such a machine when actually free from the earth. When it is considered that the machine is of great size and that it is necessary that it should move through the air at a velocity of at least 35 miles an hour in order to leave the ground, it will be obvious that manœuvring experiments cannot be conducted in a circumscribed place such as I now have. It is therefore necessary for me to obtain new and much larger premises where I shall have a very large and level field at my disposal. It is not an easy matter to obtain a field of this character in England, and it is almost impossible to find a suitable place near London. Moreover, experiments of this character, which are of little value unless conducted on a large scale, are exceedingly expensive, in fact, too expensive to be conducted by private individuals. Nevertheless, as my experiments have shown most conclusively that flying machines are not only possible but practicable, I think I am justified in continuing my experiments until a comparatively perfect flying machine has been evolved. When I have obtained possession of a suitable field, I propose to erect a large building which will contain the machine with all its wings in position. The building which I have at present, notwithstanding that it cost $15,000, is not large enough for the purpose, as the wings all have to be taken off before the machine can be housed.

There are so many points that may be improved that I have determined to build a new machine on a somewhat smaller scale, using about 200 or 250 horse-power. I shall make the engines of a longer stroke in proportion to their diameter so as to get a greater piston speed.[1] I shall construct my screw propellers with 4 long and narrow blades, very sharp and thin, and shall make them large enough so that the pressure on the projected area of the blades will be about 10 lbs. per square foot instead of over 20 lbs. as now. This will greatly reduce the

---

[1] The present piston speed does not exceed 800 feet per minute. The piston speed of express locomotives is often more than 1,000 feet per minute.

waste of power which is now lost in screw slip. As the present boiler has been found larger than is necessary, my next boiler will be made lighter and smaller, and instead of carrying a pressure of 320 lbs. to the square inch, I shall only carry 275 lbs. But the greatest improvement will be made in the framework of the machine, which will be constructed with a view of enabling everything to be driven through the air with the least possible resistance. The main aeroplane will be the same form as now, but placed at an angle of 1 in 13 instead of 1 in 8, and will be used principally for preventing the machine from accidentally falling to the earth. The principal lifting effect will be derived from a considerable number of relatively narrow aeroplanes placed on each side of the machine and mounted in such a position that the air can pass freely between them. The fore and aft rudders will be the same form as those now employed. The condenser will consist of a large number of small hollow aeroplanes about 2 inches wide, made of very thin and light metal and placed immediately behind the screw-propellers. They will be placed at such an angle as to lift about 1,000 pounds in addition to their weight and the weight of their contents. Instead of mounting my machine as now on 4 wheels, I propose to mount it on 3, the two hind wheels being about 40 feet apart and the forward wheel placed about 60 feet in front of these. I propose to lay down a track of 3 rails, the sleepers being embedded in the ground so as to produce a comparatively level surface. This railway track should be oval or circular in form so that the machine may be heavily weighed to keep it on the track and be run at a high speed. This will enable me to test the furnace draught, the burner, the steam, the boiler, the engines, the propelling effects of the screws, and the efficiency of the condenser while the machine is on the ground.

When all the machinery has been made to run smoothly I shall remove all the weight except that directly over the front wheel, and shall place a device between the wheel and the machine that will indicate the lift on the front end of the machine. I shall then run the machine over the track at a velocity which will just barely lift the hind wheels off the track, leaving the front wheel on the track. If the rear end of the machine lifts into the air it will change the angle of the planes and the lifting effect will be correspondingly diminished. This will prevent rising too high. Special wheels with a wide face suitable for running on either the rails or the earth will be provided for the purpose, and when I find that I can keep the hind wheels in the air and produce a varying lifting effect above and below the normal weight resting on the front wheel, I shall remove the weight from the forward wheel and attempt free flight by running the machine as near the ground as possible, making the first attempt by running against the wind, and it will only be after I find that I can steer my machine and manage it within a few feet of the earth, ascend and descend again at will, that I shall attempt high flight.

My experiments have certainly demonstrated that a steam engine and boiler may be made which will generate a horse-power for every six pounds of weight, and that the whole motor, including the gas generator, the water supply, the condenser, and the pumps may be all made to come inside of 11 lbs. to the horse-power. They also show that well made screw propellers working in the air are fairly efficient, and that they obtain a sufficient grip upon the air to drive the machine forward at a high velocity; that very large aeroplanes, if well made and placed at a proper angle, will lift as much as 2½ lbs. per square foot at a velocity not greater than 40 miles an hour; also that it is possible for a machine to be made so light and at the same time so powerful that it will lift not only its own weight but a considerable amount besides, with no other energy except that derived from its own engines. Therefore there can be no question but what a flying machine is now possible without the aid of a balloon in any form.

In order to obtain these results it has been necessary for me to make a great number of expensive experiments and to carefully study many of the properties of the air. Both Lord Kelvin and Lord Rayleigh, after witnessing a series of my experiments, expressed themselves as of the opinion that all the mathematical formulæ relating to planes driven through the air at an angle would have to be completely modified. Lord Kelvin himself has written that in some cases my experiments have proved that the conditions were from 20 to 50 times as favorable to the aerial navigator as had heretofore been shown by accepted formulæ, and that the whole mathematical question would require revision.

Experiments of this character unless conducted with great care are exceedingly dangerous. No makeshift or imperfect apparatus should be employed, but the experimenter should have the advantage of the most perfect appliances and apparatus that modern civilization can afford. The necessary plant for conducting experiments in a proper and safe manner is unfortunately much more expensive than the machine itself. If I find that my experiments require more money than I have at my disposal, I feel sure that some future experimenter more fortunate than myself will commence where I leave off, and with the advantages of the knowledge which has been gained by recent experiments will be able to construct a practical flying machine which cannot fail to be a great advantage to mankind.

The numerous and very expensive experiments, conducted on an unprecedented scale, which have made all this possible, and also brought to light new laws relating to the atmosphere, cannot fail to be of the greatest value to mankind, and it is on this basis that I submit the foregoing thesis.

OCTAVE CHANUTE.

(WITH PORTRAIT.)

OCTAVE CHANUTE, ex-President of the American Society of Civil Engineers, was born in Paris, France, Feb. 18, 1832, and came to the United States in the latter part of 1838. He received his education chiefly in New York City, and began the practice of his profession as a civil engineer in 1849, on the construction of the Hudson River Railroad, under JOHN B. JERVIS, Chief Engineer.

He was gradually promoted as the work progressed over the several divisions of the road, and when he left the service of that company, in 1853, he was Division Engineer at Albany, in charge of the completion of terminal facilities and maintenance of way between Hudson and Albany.

In 1853 he went to Illinois with H. A. GARDNER, previously Chief Engineer of the Hudson River Railroad, and was there engaged in building what is now a part of the Chicago & Alton Railroad, between Joliet and Bloomington, in Illinois. Mr. CHANUTE remained upon this work until 1854, when he was made Chief Engineer of the eastern portion of what is now the Toledo, Peoria, & Warsaw Railroad. He built this road from Peoria to the Indiana State line, a distance of about 112 miles, and remained in charge of maintenance of way until 1861. In the latter year he became Division Engineer, with similar duties, on the Pittsburg, Fort Wayne, & Chicago Railroad, between Chicago and Fort Wayne.

In 1862 he was for six months Chief Engineer of Maintenance of Way of the Western Division of the Ohio & Mississippi Railroad, from St. Louis to Vincennes. In 1863 he became Chief Engineer of Maintenance of Way and Construction of the re-

Plate XI.

OCTAVE CHANUTE.

Intentionally blank as was the original edition.

organized Chicago & Alton Railroad, and remained upon that line until 1867.

During this connection, having been invited to submit a design for the proposed Union Stock Yards of Chicago, his plan was selected in competition with a number of others and he built these yards as Chief Engineer. He was also awarded a premium for a competitive design for a bridge across the Missouri River at St. Charles, Missouri. In 1867 Mr. CHANUTE went to Kansas City, Mo., as Chief Engineer of the bridge across the Missouri River at that point. This was the pioneer bridge across the Missouri River, and as the river pilots and riparian dwellers had given this stream a bad reputation, the successful completion of this bridge across it in 1868 attracted great attention and interest.

Meanwhile the building of railroads had begun in Kansas, and while yet occupied in the completion of the bridge Mr. CHANUTE was placed in charge as Chief Engineer, first of the construction of the Kansas City, Fort Scott, & Gulf Railroad, from Kansas City to the north line of the Indian Territory, 160 miles; next of a parallel line in the same interest, then known as the Leavenworth, Lawrence, & Galveston Railroad, from Lawrence, Kansas, to the Indian Territory; next of a connecting line between the two, known as the Kansas City & Santa Fé Railroad, and lastly of the Atchison & Nebraska Railroad from Atchison northward.

While simultaneously in charge of the construction of these four railroads, he also designed and built the Union Stock Yards at Kansas City; and in 1871, as the work drew to a close, he became general Superintendent of the Leavenworth, Lawrence, & Galveston Railroad.

In 1873 he was offered and accepted the position of Chief Engineer of the Erie Railway, which, having changed its management, was planning to make extensive improvements. These were to consist of doubling the tracks and narrowing the gauge; building an extension to Chicago and another to Boston, involving the Poughkeepsie bridge since built in another interest; building sundry branches, and improving the property generally at an estimated outlay of some fifty millions of dollars, which it was expected to obtain in England.

The panic of 1873 and the subsequent financial depression prevented the full carrying out of this programme. Mr. CHANUTE, however, remained upon the Erie Railway 10 years, during which time much of the line was double-tracked upon improved grades, the gauge reduced to the standard by laying down a third rail, and the facilities of the line largely improved. In 1875 he was made Assistant General Superintendent, and in 1876 was placed temporarily in charge of the motive power and rolling stock, in addition to his duties as Chief Engineer. This gave him an opportunity of readjusting the locomotives as well as the grades, so that the through freight train, which averaged 18 cars when he first became connected with the line, had grown to 35 cars when he closed his connection with the road in 1883, when he removed from New York to Kansas City, in order to look after his personal interests, and to open an office as Consulting Engineer.

In this latter capacity he took charge of the construction of the iron bridges during the building of the Chicago, Burlington, & Northern Railroad between Chicago and St. Paul in 1885, and of those of the extension of the Atchison, Topeka, & Santa Fé Railroad, from Kansas City to Chicago, in 1887 and 1888; the latter involving, besides a number of minor streams, the Missouri River bridge at Sibley, and the Mississippi River bridge at Fort Madison.

In 1889 Mr. CHANUTE removed his office to Chicago, where he is now principally engaged in promoting the preservation of timber against decay by chemical methods; he being of the opinion that the time has now fully arrived when large economies are to be attained in this country by employing the methods which are in current use abroad.

Mr. CHANUTE became a member of the American Society of Civil Engineers, Feb. 19, 1868, and has contributed a goodly number of papers to its Transactions. Among these may be

mentioned, " The Elements of Cost of Railroad Freight Traffic,"
" Rapid Transit and Terminal Freight Facilities," " The Preservation of Timber," the latter two being reports by committees
of which he was chairman; " Engineering Progress in the
United States," " Repairs of Masonry," and " Uniformity in
Railroad Rolling Stock," besides some contributions to various
other societies.

The foregoing biographical sketch is reprinted from *Engineering News*, N.Y., 1891. Since it appeared, Mr. Chanute has
rendered to the cause of aeronautical science a service of the
greatest value. He has written one of the most important books[1]
on flying machines which has ever appeared; he took an active
part in the proceedings of the International Conference on
Aerial Navigation held in Chicago at the time of the World's
Fair; he has also given most generous pecuniary aid to experimenters in need of money.

His high attainments as an engineer enable him to estimate
with rare precision the value of the experiments made by others
and to show investigators just what bearing their individual
work has upon the world's work. — *Ed.*

---

[1] " Progress in Flying Machines," N. Y., 1894.

SAILING FLIGHT.

By O. Chanute.

THE soaring, or as the French term it more properly, the sailing flight (vol-à-voile) of certain species of birds, that is to say their power of progressing through the air and of translating themselves at will without any flapping action whatever, has always seemed such a mechanical paradox that its very existence has been questioned by those who have not carefully observed the performance of these birds.[1]

That a bird should float on outstretched wings high in air for hours, with no muscular exertion whatever save the passive one of keeping his wings rigidly extended, seems so preposterous, so much against all our mechanical instincts and experience of the law that expenditure of energy is necessary to produce locomotion, that even when the feat of soaring is first witnessed, the mind doubts the evidence of the eyes and seeks for some undetected movement to account for the forward advance.

Yet there is nothing more certain than that the soaring birds are supported and propelled without flap of wing. It is generally conceded by observers that they extract from the wind the energy necessary to the performance, but the exact way in which this is done is not at all agreed upon.

One principal reason why this extraordinary mode of flight has not attracted more attention, is that the performance is comparatively rare in northern latitudes. It requires a combination of favorable circumstances to entice to the locality the birds which practise it, such as regular diurnal breezes, neither too weak nor too strong, abundant food, and a mild

---

[1] The principal sailing birds are the vultures, the eagles, kites, hawks, herons, cranes, pelicans, gulls, frigate bird, and albatross.

climate. These circumstances chiefly obtain in subtropical latitudes, and in the vicinity of the sea, and in such regions the soaring birds are plentiful, while in the colder regions, where man's activities are greatest, only the eagles, the hawks, and an occasional visiting vulture are to be seen.

Buzzards and some other soaring birds are, however, abundant in the Southern United States, and much the most convincing evidence would be obtained by personal observation; but for the benefit of those readers who have never seen the performance under favorable circumstances, the following list of authors may be given, who have either described sailing-flight, or advanced theories for its explanation.

LIST OF AUTHORS.

D'Esterno. "Du vol des oiseaux." Chap. VII.

Duke of Argyle. "The reign of law." Chap. III.

L. P. Mouillard. "L'empire de l'air." "Vol des voiliers."

E. J. Marey. "Le vol des oiseaux." Chap. XX.

A. Goupil. "La locomotion aérienne." Chap. IV.

S. Drzewiecki. "Le vol plané." Pamphlet.

A. Pénaud. "Le vol-à-voile," "Aéronaute," March, 1875.

C. De Louvrié. " " " May, 1884.

J. E. Basté. " " " Sept.–Oct.–Nov., 1887.

J. Bretonnière. "Le vol plané." " June–July, 1889.

" " " " Apr.–May, 1890.

C. Weyher. " " " July, 1884.

" " " " March, 1885.

" " " " Oct., 1890.

I. Lancaster. "Soaring flight." Letters. "London Engineer," 1882.

J. C. Proctor and others. "Report, Aeronautical Society, Gt. Britain," 1880.

" Various articles in "Knowledge" and newspapers.

S. E. Peal. Aer'l Soc. 1881.' P. 10. — "Nature," May 21, 1891.

Thos. Moy.   Appendix to "Progress in flying machines." P.
271.
M. Blum. "Soaring." "R.R. and Engineers' Journal," March,
1891.
H. C. Vogt.   "   "London Engineering," March 23, 1892.
C. Darwin. "Journal on H.M.S. 'Beagle.'" Pp. 223, 224.
E. Liais. "L'espace celeste." P. 335.
Lord Rayleigh. "Soaring." Sundry letters in "Nature," 1883.
A. F. Zahm.   "   "Notre Dame Scholastic," Dec. 10,
1892.

S. P. Langley. "Internal work of wind." ⎫
J. Bretonnière. "Sailing flight."   ⎪ Proceedings
W. Kress. "Theory of flight."   ⎪ Int'l Conference
E. C. Huffaker. "Soaring flight."   ⎬ on Aerial
C. De Louvrié. "Theory of flight."   ⎪ Navigation,
A. M. Wellington. "Mechanics of flight." ⎭ 1893.
R. Soreau. "Revue Scientifique," March 30 and April 5, 1895.
O. Lilienthal.   Reports of experiments.   Sundry publications.

Singularly enough, none of the above authors save the last, and perhaps Mr. Goupil, have dwelt upon the particular wing shape of the soaring birds, or explained in their theories why certain species of birds can sail and certain others can only glide [1] (that is to say, slide over the air on fixed wings by utilizing previously acquired momentum or the force of gravity), while the sailing birds can extract from the wind all the energy needed for support or propulsion.

This seems to require a certain mass, say, from a pound's weight upward, to equate the irregularities of the wind, and a particular conformation of bird to extract energy from the

---

[1] To remove misconstructions it is well to define various modes of flight, the writer proposes the following terms:

Rowing flight. — Ordinary progression by flapping. — Examples: Ducks, Geese, etc.
Hovering "   Remaining over one fixed point. — "   Humming Birds.
Gliding "   Sliding over the air on fixed wings. — "   Pigeons, Swallows.
Soaring "   Sailing with occasional flaps. — "   Hawks, Eagles, etc.
Sailing "   Utilizing the wind alone. — "   Excelled in by Vultures, Albatross, etc.

wind to the best advantage, so that the main conditions of
sailing flight seem to be:

1. There must be wind, although it may be light.
2. No flapping whatever is needed when under way.
3. The bird must have a peculiar conformation.
4. The bird needs a certain mass or weight.

Few of the above-named authors give any precise measurements, so that it is impossible to test their theories by numer-
ical examples and computations. The writer was thereby
induced to gather such data for himself. He now proposes,
first, to give the results of some of his observations, and then
to attempt to reduce the data to the sway of mathematical laws.

PART I. — THE OBSERVATIONS.

In the Southern United States the sailing bird most frequently seen is the turkey-buzzard (Cathartes aura). He is
an accomplished soarer, but is somewhat inaccessible, so that
it is difficult to watch his manœuvres at close range. The
frigate-bird and the pelican are generally still higher up in air
or more distant, so that while it is easy to become entirely satisfied that while sailing they obtain all their support and motion
without flapping their wings, it is more difficult to observe just
how they do it.

After watching many of these birds in Texas, Louisiana, and
Florida, the writer found that his desire for exact observations
was best gratified by the gulls of California; and omitting here-
in therefore all the other observations made of other species of
birds at longer range, he proposes to confine his relation to the
acts of birds which he could watch currently at fifteen to twenty
feet distance.

The gulls of San Diego (California) are extraordinarily tame.
They are not suffered to be molested, because they act as scav-
engers of floating refuse food about the harbor, and while the
greater number of their kind live out in the open sea, upon fish
and the slop of passing vessels, the knowing ones dwell in the
bay and feed upon the broken victuals thrown from ships, and

upon the garbage of the city. They wait for "Steamer day" with all the eagerness of old Californians before the days of railways, and when a craft comes in they congregate about it on the wing, awaiting the refuse from the kitchen.

They are absolutely fearless of man, and will float or fly within 15 to 30 feet of him while performing their evolutions, so that more may be learned of the minute acts of soaring from them in an hour than from months of observations of other birds which soar comparatively high in the air. Indeed, it is possible to detect their every motion, however slight, to see how they get started underway, how they glide or sail, how they balance themselves in a variable wind, and how they stop their headway to alight. When they sail, there can be no question of there being undetected movements, for the wings are absolutely rigid, the operation being often performed in such close proximity to the observer that the fluttering of a stray bit of down, protruding from below the secondary feathers, can be plainly seen.

By either standing on the lower, or on the middle, or on the upper deck of a steamer, the gulls can be watched either from below, or on a level with the eye, or from above, as may be preferred, so that one observation shall check another concerning the same act of manœuvring.

These acts, for the present purpose (which does not concern itself with rowing flight), may be divided under four heads:

      1st. Starting, or getting under way.
      2d. Sailing, or soaring on the wind.
      3d. Balancing, or maintaining the equilibrium.
      4th. Alighting, including stopping the motion.

It may be well to state here, for the benefit of those whose observations have been confined to rowing birds, that while during the first few vigorous strokes, the weight is all sustained by the reaction of the downward blow of the wing on the air, as soon as forward motion is obtained the bird acts as an aeroplane, and the support is mainly or all derived from the air pressure due to the forward speed ; that is to say, that the under surface of the wings, whether flapping or extended rigidly, and when progressing as an inclined plane, receives a pressure from the impinging air which acts at right angles to the surface. This pressure is resolved into two components, one vertical which sustains the weight, and the other horizontal which either opposes the motion, if the angle of incidence be above the horizon, or acts as a propelling force if the angle be inclined below the horizon. Thus the flappings of the wings (which the investigations of Professor Marey show to be delivered at a varying angle) chiefly serve as a propelling force when the bird is under full headway, and the bird may also be sustained when gliding or sailing upon rigidly extended wings, provided he have headway enough. In still-air gliding this headway has to be furnished by gravity or from previous momentum, but in sailing the same effect is produced by the passing wind, provided it has sufficient motion with respect to the bird.

Sailing flight depends upon this latter condition, and as the wind constantly varies in intensity, as was well shown by Professor Langley, a certain amount of momentum or mass is required to perform sailing flight properly, and hence it is best exhibited by the larger and heavier birds.

It thus appears that the first important thing for the bird to accomplish in order that he may soar, is to acquire and to retain initial velocity, so that he may at all times, against the wind or with the wind, obtain support from the air by glancing over it at a sufficient speed and angle to produce a sustaining pressure. The first manœuvre to observe, therefore, is how he obtains this initial velocity, and the following comprise the results of the writer's observations of gulls at San Diego.

STARTING.

The gulls take their start either from the surface of the water or from a perch.

If from the former, they first face the wind, paddle a few strokes, spring from the water into the air and flap vigorously for a time, flying directly against the wind and nearly on a level course, some 4 to 6 feet above the water. The flaps at first average 3 per second, and are of great amplitude, or nearly half of a circle, but as headway is gained, say in a distance of 20 to 30 feet, the amplitude is reduced to about 45°, each side of the wing pivot, and the number of strokes gradually diminishes to 2 per second, and eventually to 1 stroke per second, the bird rising meanwhile at an angle rather less than 45°, to a height of 30 or 40 feet above the water, this altitude being gained in a course of 150 to 200 feet, at the end of which the velocity of the bird (measured in still air) is from 26 to 30 feet per second, when, if the wind be sufficient, he is in good condition for soaring flight.

If the gull be on a perch (and the bird seems much to prefer this position), say on the ridge of a building, on the edge of a wharf, or on a pile-head, his exertions to start are much less. He faces the wind as before, launches himself forward and downward, gaining impetus from gravity, and with a very few flaps — sometimes without any — he acquires a velocity of 26 feet per second, then he rises and is prepared to soar upon the wind, which is evidently more rapid at a height of 30 or 40 feet above the water than it is at the surface. The bird may alternately flap and glide for a few seconds, but as soon as he feels himself in a sufficiently strong current, say of 18 to 20 feet per second, he ceases all active exertions and abandons himself wholly to the pleasures of sailing.

If the breeze be steady and strong enough, say 19 to 22 measured feet per second at the surface of the wharf, the gulls occasionally exhibit a third and very remarkable method of getting under way.

This is sometimes performed from the ridge of a building, or from a ship's spar, but the most satisfactory observations are obtained when the bird is on a pile-head about 10 feet above the water, and therefore on a level with the eye of the observer on the wharf, and some 15 or 20 feet distant. The writer has seen the feat performed many times and will describe the best instances.

The bird stands on the pile-head, and faces the wind. He opens his wing wide, but keeps the front edges depressed, so that the wind glances over them and presses him downward;

then, when the breeze freshens, he changes the plane of his wings by a slight twist, until they present an angle of incidence of about 20° above the horizon. The wind, pressing under the wings, lifts the bird up 2 or 3 feet. The first part of this ascent is quite vertical, but presently the gull, still rising, drifts back about 5 feet, when he comes to a poise for an instant as he changes his angle of incidence, so that it becomes negative and points below the horizon, when his course is reversed. He plunges downward and against the wind until he is within about 4 feet of the water, when, having acquired an initial speed of his own, of about 26 feet per second, he again changes his angle of incidence to some 12° or 15° above the horizon, and he rises again, and is henceforth master of his movements, continuing to sail without flapping, apparently in any direction he desires.

The wind, on the occasions when this performance was exhibited, blew with comparative steadiness at a speed of 14 to 23 feet per second, with an average of 21.12 ft. per second, or 14.4 miles per hour. The sea breeze at San Diego sprang up every morning, being caused by the rarefaction of the air in the sun over the California deserts, and during the writer's visit the wind blew every day from the same quarter and with nearly the same intensity, making this location an ideal one for the performance of sailing flight.

Thus it is seen, that by this last starting manœuvre, it is in the power of a soaring bird, if the wind serves, to rise from his perch without flapping, to remain aloft indefinitely, as will be more particularly described under the head of Sailing, and to return to a perch again, *without furnishing a single stroke of wing*. In point of fact the birds not infrequently give a flap or two, but this seems to be done more as a matter of convenience, to trim the course, or to maintain the velocity.

SAILING.

Once well underway, with their own speed of 26 to 30 feet per second (17.7 to 20.4 miles per hour), the gulls seem to be master of their movements, and, if the breeze blows from 14 to

23 ft. per second (12.92 to 15.64 miles per hour), to be able to translate themselves to any point they choose.

The manœuvre ·which can be observed at closest range consists in patrolling at lunch time along the water side of a steamer tied to the wharf. The birds then sail back and forth along the side, at a distance of 20 to 30 ft. therefrom and at a height of about 30 ft. above the water. They are attending upon the cook, in hope of garbage.

On the occasion at which the most satisfactory measurements were made the gulls sailed along back and forth a distance of about 100 ft. parallel with the steamer, and some 20 ft. therefrom, so that from the middle deck they could be looked in the eye and the least movement detected. They floated on a horizontal course, turning upon their heel at the end of each lap, and returning over the same path. This was done entirely without beat of wing, or tremor of a feather, save an occasional fluttering of a bit of down projecting from beneath ill-matched feathers, and it entirely set at rest in the mind of the writer any assumption as to support being gained from any minute movements of the feathers or tail.

Whenever a bucket of slops was emptied from the kitchen, the gulls wheeled at once, poised themselves for an instant, and swooped down towards the food. When within 5 ft. of the water they began a curve, throwing their wings at an angle into the attitude of an obtuse angle, and describing nearly a semicircle, they snapped up a mouthful from the water. Then they remounted with a few vigorous flaps, to a soaring attitude on a level with the upper deck of the steamer; thence, a fresh poise having been obtained, and the food swallowed, the operation would be repeated, and when all the slop was eaten up, the sailing along the side would be resumed until the next bucketful.

The wind was blowing at an observed mean velocity (6 measurements) of 18.83 ft. per second, or 12.78 miles per hour, and at an angle of 30° (as near as could be judged) with the line of the ship. The gulls progressed against this side wind at a measured speed of 10 ft. per second, with reference to the ship, and their speed with reference to the wind was therefore equal to its velocity, multiplied by the cosine of the angle of incidence, plus their own apparent motion. Hence the relative speed was $18.83 \times 0.866 + 10 = 26.3$ ft. per second, or 17.88 miles per hour. At this speed the birds were perfectly sustained, and floated back and forth on extended wings slightly arched, wheeling with a short turn at the end of each course, their heads turning from side to side, and their little eyes eagerly watching. Their angle of incidence above the horizon was $5°$ to $7°$, as near as it could be measured when going against the wind, but this angle of incidence is very difficult of measurement, and moreover it constantly varies with the speed, or when the bird rises or falls, or goes with or against the wind. It was estimated by holding a pencil on the line of the water horizon.

During all the time, the birds were constantly balancing themselves, as will be more fully explained hereafter, so that it must not be understood that when they are spoken of as floating on the breeze, they made no movements whatever to regulate their poise or angle of incidence, or to counteract the variations in the direction and intensity of the air currents. Such movements were, however, very slight, about as active as those made by a man to balance himself in walking, and clearly they did not furnish any motive-power for support or propulsion. This power all came from the wind, as will be more fully discussed when the attempt is made to account mathematically for the phenomenon.

There being a question as to the horizontality of the wind, this was tested by liberating bits of tissue paper (such as that placed between visiting cards), from the edge of the steamer. The wind blew them upward at various angles, generally from $10°$ to $20°$; so that it was concluded that the side of the ship produced an ascending trend in the wind; what that trend was at the birds, 20 feet away, there was no mode of ascertaining, but it is believed that it materially assisted them in their evolutions.

Meantime, in other parts of the harbor, other gulls were observed patrolling the sky. They generally soared higher in the air, at a height of 100 to 200 feet, probably to avail of the stronger breeze prevailing at that height, and presumably blowing with exact horizontality. With these latter birds the favorite course seemed to be quartering with the wind, back and forth, for 500 to 800 feet. Their relative speed, after allowing for that of the wind, seemed, by measurement, to be from 22 to 24 feet per second, but the writer believes it to have been somewhat more, as the wind was measured at the surface of a dock, while the birds were aloft. On some mornings, before the sea breeze had fully set in, and when the wind was consequently light, a favorite course seemed to lie just above and to the leeward of a set of " coal pockets " on a dock, which forms a wind-break 650 feet long and about 25 feet high, thus lending additional countenance to the theory that a soaring bird finds assistance from ascending currents of air, deflected from their horizontal course by some obstacle or by rising ground; but when the wind grew stronger, the gulls soared indifferently all over the harbor.

At other times the gulls circled in the air, gradually drifting to leeward. These circlings were seldom long continued, and lacked the majesty of the great sweeps of the buzzard when surveying a township from aloft. The gulls circle rather irregularly, but observation indicated that they dropped earthward while sailing with the wind, thus gaining speed from gravity, and rose more than they had dropped when they reached the quarter circle performed against the wind, thus utilizing the increased velocity to regain the lost altitude. At times, they seemed poised, absolutely fixed in one spot, their own initial velocity at that time being of course exactly equal to that of the wind, and at other times they rose upwards but drifted backward, a little gust of wind having apparently furnished a surplus of sustaining power, but at the expense of forward motion.

In one or two rare instances, the birds were seen both to rise and to advance in a straight line against the wind simultaneously, and this is the hardest manœuvre to explain mathematically. It has, however, been well described and figured by M.

Basté, and his diagrams will be used when an attempt is made to account for this paradox.

The birds having no particular motive to demonstrate that they can sail indefinitely without flapping, occasionally resort to the latter in their manœuvres. When gliding or sailing upon the breeze, they perform an occasional flap, a mere kick, as it were, either to limber up the outstretched wings, or to maintain the speed they require to obtain a sustaining reaction, or to overcome the head resistance without changing their angle of incidence when the wind chances to weaken. Sometimes, also, they glide down some distance and gain speed at the expense of height, to be recovered when the breeze freshens; but there is nothing more certain in the writer's mind than the fact that wind is required for sailing flight, and that the few observers who claim to have seen soaring performed in a dead calm, must in some way have been mistaken.

By a calm, or by a very light breeze of 2 to 4 miles per hour, such as generally prevails in the early morning hours at San Diego, sailing flight does not seem to be performable by the gulls, and if they want to go somewhere they flap exclusively. Their speed when flapping in a calm is from 30 to 33 ft. per second (20.4 to 22.44 miles per hour), this being the result of many measurements along distances of 350 to 500 ft. The harbor gulls are lazy birds, however, and evidently dislike the exertion, for, during a dead calm, most of their time is spent on firm support, the favorite places being the outer ends of piers with little traffic, where there is a chance for the birds to walk about and squawk, apparently in gossip with each other.

When the sea-breeze springs up, generally before noon, the more active or hungry gulls start out upon a cruise, and by rowing flight, continued until they are high in the air, find a wind sufficiently strong for them to sail in, and when this has freshened to 11 or 15 miles an hour at the dock surface, all the gulls leave their perch and float upon the breeze, sailing then seeming to be preferred by them to perching, as involving no more exertion and being a pleasanter mode of passing the time, even when a meal is no longer a desideratum.

If, however, the wind increases to over 30 miles an hour (a rare occurrence), the gulls seem to find sailing unpleasant and generally seek some quiet spot, more or less sheltered, to allow the storm to blow over.

The greatest exertion performed by the gulls is, apparently, during the act of hovering, when beating their wings rapidly so as to remain at a fixed point just above the water, to inspect closely a suspicious morsel. The body is then held at an angle of about 40° with the water, some 18 or 24 inches above it, and the wings are vibrated fast, though without a great amplitude, while the bird remains several seconds in one spot, and cranes his neck forward. If the morsel be deemed acceptable, he sweeps down, snatches it in his beak, and with much flutter, balancing, and effort, he rises again with vigorous flaps to resume his soaring flight, generally preferring, however, to do this at an angle of 30° to 45° to the wind, back and forth, so as to convey to the observer the idea that he is making a series of tacks against the wind.

Almost all observers are agreed (D'Esterno, Mouillard, Pénaud, De Louvrié, Basté, Bretonnière, Proctor, Peal, Langley, etc.) that wind is absolutely necessary for the performance of sailing flight. All of the observations of the writer confirm this, although he has seen the feat performed by buzzards and by hawks, when the breeze measured only 5 or 6 miles an hour at the surface. It may have been more rapid higher up, where the bird was. The gulls do not seem to soar well unless the wind blows at about 10 miles per hour. The difference is probably accounted for by the difference in proportion of carrying surface to the weight, this being, according to the writer's measurements, very nearly 1 lb. to the square foot for the gull, while it is 0.88 lb. per square foot for the buzzard and 0.55 lb. per square foot for the chicken-hawk.

Before making the observations above described a " herring gull " had been shot, weighed, and measured. Its weight was 2.188 lbs., its entire surface, wings, tail, and body projected, measured 2.015 square feet, its cross-section of body at the maximum point was 0.126 square feet, and its cross-section of wings, projected at the point of maximum anterior thickness, was 0.098 square feet. These figures will hereafter be used in computing the support and resistances.

All sailing birds are accomplished acrobats. It is difficult to detect the more minute movements in the hawks, the buzzards, the frigate-bird, etc., which generally sail at a considerable altitude, but they can be closely studied in the fearless gulls of San Diego, which perform their evolutions right under the observer's nose.

As the wind varies in intensity, or as the birds wish to rise or to fall, they are constantly changing their angle of incidence and their poise. This is done by advancing or moving to the rear the tips of the wings, which are stretched out in a soaring attitude. The movement is slight, and, as the writer suspects, is also automatic. It alters the poise at once fore and aft, and the bird either rises or falls, or he restores the adjustment between his own speed and that of the wind.

If he wants to wheel to one side, a manœuvre which is done very gracefully, he apparently increases the flexion of the wing on the side to which he wants to turn, the body tilts to that side in consequence of its disturbed balance, and the bird wheels to that side. The same result is also thought to follow the advancing of one wing more than the other, but the writer does not feel that his observations are quite conclusive on that point.

But most of the continual balancing is effected with the head and the feet, which, when the wind is at all gusty, are almost constantly in action. The fore and aft balancing is sometimes effected with the head alone, the neck being stretched out or drawn in, or it may be swung from side to side to preserve the transverse equilibrium. Often, however, the legs also come into action. When in full sailing activity in a steady breeze, they are rigidly extended out back under the tail, but when a gust of wind compromises the balance, the legs drop downward, making an angle at the knee, and the feet are adjusted as required to preserve the fore and aft balance, by altering the leverage due to their weight, making thus an adjustable pendule of great efficiency.

As has been said, these movements are slight, and hence difficult to detect except at very close range; nor are they continual, as they are only made as occasion requires, without apparently taking more thought than a man does while walking. They are doubtless due to reflex action as guided by acquired instinct, but they point out the enormous difficulties to be encountered by man if he seeks to imitate the bird, and to sail upon the gusty wind, before he has acquired the science of balancing, or produced an automatic apparatus of his own.

It is difficult to determine accurately the angle of incidence which the bird makes with the horizon when sailing. The general plane of the wings does not seem to be parallel with the lower edge of the body, and the eye becomes confused in estimating the angle. This angle, moreover, constantly varies with the speed, within small limits, but the writer deems it to range between 3° and 15° above the horizon when the bird is on a level course. As he rises or falls the angle of incidence is materially altered, both above and below the horizon, but from the best projections made by the writer against the sky line, he deems that the most usual angle of the wings, when sailing upon a level course, is from 5° to 7° above the horizon, and the latter figure will be used in the mathematical computations.

One peculiarity of the sailing gull consists in his attitude, — the wings are arched downward like a bow. Land-sailing birds generally hold their wings extended either horizontally, or so as to make with each other a slight diedral angle above the horizon, while the gulls and many other sea birds hold their wings when sailing in the singular position described. Why this should be so the writer has been unable to surmise.

ALIGHTING.

While the manœuvres performed in alighting exhibit as many varieties as those for starting, they can be described briefly. The object of the bird is evidently to stop his forward motion so as to avoid a shock upon alighting, and this is very neatly performed in a variety of ways. The method preferred is to arrive at the point selected at a lower level and to rise to the perch, thus destroying speed by the action of gravity. The bird generally rises some 18 inches above the selected perch, this rise being performed at an angle of about 45° or more, and then he poises for an instant and gently drops feet downward on the perch. Sometimes the arriving course is on a level with the point selected; in that case the bird tilts himself to an angle of some 40° to the line of motion and without beat of wing, if he has calculated just right, he finds his headway stopped just above the perch and drops down to it as previously described.

Or the motion may be stopped by backward beat of wing, or by hovering with vibrating wings just above the spot selected, so that the pendant legs soon touch the perch, or the gull's body settles upon the water, but in every case the bird contrives to arrive from such a direction that he faces the wind, if any, when at the perch, and utilizes this as a retarding force.

These are the observations. They were made in March, 1892, and written out in full at the time, substantially as now published, but it took me three years to arrive at a satisfactory explanation of what I had seen, and to compute the forces in action. The chief trouble was that the calculations of weights sustained, at the observed speeds and angles of incidence, were based upon the known pressures of air upon plane surfaces, adding, however, a coefficient obtained, with a pigeon's wing, a non-soaring bird. It was only when Herr Lilienthal's table of air pressures was obtained, in the " Handbook for Aeronauts and Aviators " [1] that I was enabled to figure up satisfactory reactions, with the coefficients obtained by actual experiments with surfaces shaped like the wings of sailing birds.

---

[1] " Taschenbuch für Flugtechniker und Luftschiffer." 1895. W. H. Kuhl, 73 Jägerstrasse, Berlin W.

NOTE. — Mr. Chanute not having yet had leisure to prepare the text to accompany his computations, has somewhat reluctantly consented to the present publication of this first part. He intends soon to follow it with the mathematical demonstration, and this may be published in a Supplement to the Annual. — *Editor.*

HOW A BIRD SOARS.

By Professor William H. Pickering, of Harvard Observatory.

By "soaring" is meant the upward spiral progress of a bird, without apparent muscular effort. This action may be observed in this part of the world to particular advantage, in the case of certain large hawks. The following explanation of the principle of soaring is extracted from an article which I published in "Science," 1889, p. 245, and is, I believe, the first description of the process which ascribes to gusts of wind their true influence in the production of the phenomenon:

" Whenever there is a high wind, such as is undoubtedly required by a soaring bird, we know that the air pressure is not uniform, that the wind comes in gusts. Those familiar with mountain summits know that the same phenomena are observed in the upper atmosphere as at the surface of the ground. If we were travelling along with such a wind in a balloon, the gusts would not be so severe, but they would be of longer duration.

$$A \underline{\hspace{5cm}} B$$

" Imagine, now, a bird travelling from A to B, in the same direction as the wind, and with its mean velocity. When the wind is uniform, it seems to him that he is in a dead calm. When a gust comes, the wind seems to blow from A. It carries him along faster; and when it ceases the wind seems to blow from B. It therefore affects him precisely as if he were in an alternating current of wind.

" Suppose, now, that he is drifting towards B with a velocity equal to that of the wind, and travelling at right angles to AB with such a velocity that he can move along horizontally without falling towards the earth. Suddenly a gust overtakes him

(77)

from the direction of A. He at once turns towards it, and his velocity relative to it is sufficient to raise him in the air. It tends to carry him more rapidly towards B; and when his velocity relative to it has sunk to the same value as before, and he again travels horizontally, he turns again at right angles to the line AB, but in the opposite direction to that which he had before. Presently the force of the gust diminishes, and the wind seems to blow towards him from the direction B. He accordingly turns toward it again, rising from the ground till his velocity relative to the air has assumed its former value, and he moves horizontally, turning again at right angles to the line AB, and the cycle is completed. He thus moves along in the direction AB with a mean velocity equal to that of the wind, rising when moving parallel to it, and moving horizontally, or perhaps slowly falling, if the gusts do not come with sufficient frequency, when moving at right angles to it.

"In the case of all soaring birds, the spread tail, being an inclined curved surface, presents a large area to the wind. As it is situated at a considerable distance from the bird's centre of gravity, it must convert him into a sort of floating weather-cock, the wings serving as dampers to restrain him from turning too quickly. It therefore appears, if soaring really does depend on the interaction of varying wind-currents, as if the changes of direction involved must be almost automatic, and not a thing which the bird is required to learn; although he may doubtless learn to take advantage of favoring currents by giving proper inclinations to his wings and tail.

"If the question be raised as to the sufficiency of the varying intensity of the wind-currents to maintain the bird's initial velocity against the resistance of the air, we must reply that it is a matter which can only be determined conclusively by experiment. Certain it is, however, that in windy weather the wind does come in gusts. If in the course of his circles the bird happens to be travelling at right angles to the wind, when the gust strikes him he will surely be turned round, almost in spite of himself, so as to face the gust. If the bird does face the gust, it will certainly raise him to a higher level.

" If this explanation proves to be the true one, the reason why small birds cannot soar is probably, that, in those of them that have suitably shaped wings and bodies, their surfaces are so large in proportion to their weights that they rapidly assume the velocity of the surrounding air. In order that they might soar to advantage, the gusts should come more frequently, and be of shorter duration, than we actually find to occur in nature."

Obviously, if the mean velocity of the wind is high, and the gusts comparatively insignificant, the bird may rise without difficulty, but he will drift rapidly along in the direction towards which the wind is blowing. Let us now imagine the conditions reversed; let the mean velocity of the wind be very low, while the gusts are of great intensity. The bird will now rise rapidly, and may then take advantage of his position to soar downwards against the wind, not merely holding his own, but even advancing against it. We thus see how it would be theoretically possible upon a windy day for a bird to travel at will in any desired direction without making the slightest mechanical exertion whatever, and also without taking advantage of any upward currents that might exist. That these currents do exist in certain localities, especially in hilly districts, and that they are often used by the birds almost like stairways there now seems no reason to doubt. That such upward currents are not absolutely necessary, however, for purposes of soaring, it is the object of this article to point out.

SENATE BILL, No. 302.

FIFTY-FOURTH CONGRESS.

By the Editor.

A BILL, of which the following is a copy, was introduced in the Senate of the United States on the 4th of December, 1895, by Mr. Lodge. It was read twice and referred to the Committee on Interstate Commerce.

A BILL TO SECURE AERIAL NAVIGATION.

"*Be it enacted by the Senate and House of Representatives of the United States of America in Congress assembled*, That the Secretary of the Treasury is hereby authorized and directed to pay the sum of one hundred thousand dollars to any person from whatever part of the world, who shall, at any time prior to the first day of January, nineteen hundred and one, construct an apparatus that will, on the verified report of a committee of three members appointed by the Secretary of War, demonstrate, within or near the city of Washington, the practicability of safely navigating the air at a speed of not less than thirty miles an hour, and capable of carrying passengers and freight weighing a total of at least four hundred pounds.

" SECT. 2. That the Secretary of the Treasury is hereby authorized and directed to pay the sum of twenty-five thousand dollars to any person, from whatever part of the world, who shall, at any time prior to the first day of January, nineteen hundred, construct an apparatus that will, on the verified report of a committee of three members appointed by the Secretary of War, demonstrate, within or near the city of Washington, the practicability of safely navigating the air in free flight toward any desired point of the compass for a distance of one mile or more in a descending line ; the point of alighting to be not more than sixty-six feet lower than the point of starting. No use shall be made of the buoyant power of any gas lighter than air."

In December, 1893, two years earlier than the introduction of this bill in the Senate, a bill (S. 1344) "to secure Aerial Navigation" was introduced by Mr. Cockrell, and referred to the Committee on Interstate Commerce. The earlier bill having failed to receive a recommendation from the committee to which it was referred, the editor of the Annual has drafted the present bill, and Senator Lodge has kindly complied with the request to present it to the Senate. The bill is now in the hands of the Committee on Interstate Commerce, and our present task is to induce that committee to report favorably upon it.

The earlier bill was so exacting in its requirements that, even if it had passed, there would probably have been few to compete for the prize offered. Moreover, it offered no encouragement to the designers of soaring-machines. For years the present writer has been trying to convince people of the extreme importance of the development of the motorless soaring-machine.

This bill seems likely to bring hundreds of contestants into the field, and it tends to serve the double purpose of advancing the cause of science and of providing recreation for the people.

There are two important points to be considered :

I.   The need of the passage of this bill.

II.   The probability of its accomplishing the intended result.

I.

It is needless to advert to the fact that a universal highway would be a boon to humanity, for that is generally recognized.

There are many reasons for thinking that the problem of aerial navigation can be solved before the close of the present century, if the United States government encourages investigation and experiment. When we consider the great progress which, during the present century, has been made in other sciences and useful arts, we see plainly how the science and the

useful art of aerial navigation have, until recently, been languish-
ing since the days of Cayley, who experimented and wrote well
in the early part of the century (1800–1809).

The science of aerial navigation may properly be called *the
neglected science*.

Unless the navigation of the air by man be, in the nature of
things, impossible, there surely must exist some peculiar set of
conditions which will account for man's failure to progress in
this direction as he has in others. This will briefly be pointed
out.

Until the last decade of our century, there has been a wide-
spread and unreasoning belief in the absurdity of attempts to
navigate the air. This has discouraged investigation. In consequence of the lack of educational facilities in this specialty,
investigators have been left to work on wrong lines, or by faulty
methods. Inventors and investigators are, as a rule, men of
limited means; the cost of wreckage obtains as a larger factor
in the research we are considering than in almost any other.
All these conditions are peculiar, and they account for slow
progress.

II.

As to the probability of the bill's accomplishing the intended
result: The first section of the bill explains itself. The stipu-
lations are such that neither the whole nor any part of the one
hundred thousand dollars would be expended by the United
States, save for a full solution of the problem.

The second section of the bill is for the purpose of encourag-
ing experiments which, in the absence of any government award,
would probably be comparatively unremunerative, yet which
are likely to be very important in the way of leading toward
the full solution.

The descent of sixty-six feet in one mile is permitted, in order
that men may be encouraged to familiarize themselves with the
motions of aerial travel without being put to the great expense
of providing motors.

When the useful arts of designing and controlling soaring-machines [1] have been further advanced, the expense entailed by the wreckage of valuable motors will be greatly reduced.

The grade of sixty-six feet to a mile has been fixed upon by assuming that the amount of energy required in a soaring-machine is no greater than that required to keep a railway car in motion upon a gently descending steel track.

If the total weight of a soaring-machine and its operator is two hundred pounds, and if the operator carries his machine to a height of sixty-six feet above a level plain or a sheet of water, he will have stored, within himself and his machine, potential energy amounting to 13,200 foot pounds.

We may have some idea of the transporting power of this energy if we imagine a traveller with a sled upon the glassy surface of a frozen lake tilted to a grade of sixty-six feet to the mile. We cannot yet figure the comparative air-resistances encountered by the travellers upon the ice road and upon the air road, but we have many reasons for thinking that the potential energy of a traveller starting from the summit of an air incline will carry him a surprisingly long distance.

If an experimenter wishes to make use of greater power, there is no stipulation in the bill which prevents his making a start at a high velocity, but, after making this start, the descent to a finish-mark at a distance of a mile must not exceed sixty-six feet. It is expected that the flight will be undulatory, velocity will at times be sacrificed to gain altitude, and altitude will at times be sacrificed to gain velocity, according to the existing conditions of the wind.

Several eminent scientists have expressed the opinion that motors which are now in existence are sufficiently light and powerful to propel flying-machines if the machines can be safely guided; yet as a marine engine would be useless without a properly designed hull and the ability to steer the ship clear of the land, so no motor seems likely to propel a flying-machine in free flight until man has completely mastered the motorless soaring-machine and so provided a ship for the engine.

---

[1] Soaring-machine. A motorless machine used for sailing on air.

We have in the achievements of Otto Lilienthal, of Berlin (described elsewhere in this Annual), the best of reasons for thinking that the soaring experiments which will be encouraged by the passage of this bill will lead to the final solution of this great problem, which is to the human race a matter of profound concern.

Lilienthal has made many flights in a slightly descending line, and in some of these has covered a linear distance of several hundred metres. The improvement of machines of the Lilienthal type must result in a continual lessening of the angle of descent in sailing flight. Finally, slow as has been the progress in this line of research during the past eighty years, recognition and encouragement of this science by the United States government would probably establish it in a position where rapid advancement would be possible.

THE BOSTON AERONAUTICAL SOCIETY.

THE Boston Aeronautical Society was organized May 2, 1895. Prof. William H. Pickering, of Harvard Observatory, was chosen president, and Mr. Albert A. Merrill, secretary.

The membership is at present limited to twenty. For several months fortnightly meetings have been held, and at these meetings papers treating of aeronautical subjects have been read and discussed. The members have found these discussions decidedly instructive and helpful.

Preparations are being made for many interesting experiments, which will be tried at the field meetings of the Society, to be held during the coming summer and autumn.

Nearly all of the members are active experimenters; these men feel assured that the Society has a useful work before it, and that the field will be an ever-widening one.

THE BOSTON AERONAUTICAL SOCIETY'S EXPERIMENT FUND.

LIKE many other organizations, the Boston Aeronautical Society must have money, and a good deal of it, too, in order to carry on its work.

It is now gathering a fund to be used in the encouragement of experiment with aerial machines.

The members at present, besides giving their time to the work, are giving what money they can afford. More is needed, and all who are interested in the advancement of science are invited to contribute in sums either large or small.

Any remittances sent to the Treasurer of the Boston Aeronautical Society, Box 344, Boston, Mass., will be gratefully acknowledged. (See blanks at the end of this volume.)

Contributors will desire to know what use is to be made of their money.

The members of the Society will not be satisfied until they have established a country laboratory where well-paid men may be continuously employed in experimenting.

For a building there is needed a barn-like structure near the centre of a level tract, with a large sheet of water not far away. Such a building will answer the twofold purpose of a workshop and a place for the storage of apparatus. A small captive-balloon outfit is needed, so that on any calm day small models of soaring-machines can be launched from a height. A revolving slope, as invented and described [1] by Mr. Merrill, should

---

[1] See page 102.

also be provided, so that experiments by athletes on machines of the Lilienthal type may soon be begun.

For the year 1896 a part of the money raised will be paid out to the world's experimenters in the form of cash prizes. These are to be awarded for certain kinds of apparatus which are much needed.   Specifications are given below.

The sum of money already guaranteed to the fund is sufficient to provide prizes well worth contending for, but, as it is hoped that the fund will be constantly increased, the definite announcement of the amounts of the prizes will be made public on the first of May, 1896.

The competitive trials will probably take place at a field-meeting of the Society to be held late in the autumn of 1896 in the vicinity of Boston.

Designers unable to attend are invited to send apparatus, which will be tested by a committee of the Society, according to instructions furnished by the designers.

The code of rules governing the trials and awards will be announced later.

It is hoped that experimenters from all parts of the world will enter this competition.

Those who are considering the matter of entering will be in the way of receiving full information concerning details, if they will fill out Blank No. 1 at the end of this volume.

The following prizes, five in number, are offered:

PRIZE A.   For the kite showing the maximum of lift to the minimum of drift in a breeze having a velocity of more than fifteen miles per hour.

PRIZE B.   For the kite showing the maximum of lift to the minimum of drift in a breeze having a velocity of less than fifteen miles per hour.

PRIZE C.   For the kite keeping its equilibrium through the greatest extremes of wind velocity.

PRIZE D.   For the soaring-machine in free flight, which, after gaining velocity, shall make the best course.   The excellence of the course to be judged by the maximum of length and the minimum of undulation.   Energy may be given to the machine by carrying it to a height.

PRIZE E.   For the best self-propelled machine.

The rules given are general ones only ; the interpretation will rest with the judges.   Details will be given later.

The committee in charge reserves the right to postpone the time of the competitive trials.

The foregoing stands approved.

Signed,

WILLIAM H. PICKERING,
ALBERT A. MERRILL,
JAMES MEANS,

Executive Committee of the Boston Aeronautical Society.

DYNAMIC FLIGHT.

By A. M. HERRING.

ADVANCE in a new science is generally slow, through lack of sufficient and properly interpreted data upon which to base new experiment. In flying-machine work this is especially true, for not only is there a scarcity of accurately recorded experiments, but even to get at the facts of these, we have, in most cases, to " wade backward," as it were, through a considerable amount of false interpretation of the phenomena observed.

Unfortunately the records of the work which has been done were until quite recently widely scattered; even now they are incomplete, except in a few instances where systematic series of experiments have been made by thoroughly competent physicists.

Starting with a knowledge of what is now known of the action of air on planes, it is quite easy, in a theoretical consideration of the subject, to prove that dynamic flight is not only possible with light and powerful machinery, but that the power required at high speed is so small as nearly to bring flight within the limit of man's unaided strength. But theoretical considerations omit many of the conditions which have to be met in practice. In the actual machine the conditions which arise cause a necessary waste of power many times greater than that originally allowed in even very liberal estimates. It would probably be surprising to a great many to be told that out of perhaps fifty or sixty different kinds of aeroplane and vertical screw models worked by twisted rubber, compressed air, or steam, that have been built and exhibited in flight, not more than two or three have required less than $\frac{1}{20}$ of a horse-power per pound of their weight, and that the majority required nearly twice as much, or over half the energy of a man to sustain a pound.

Yet it is a common thing to find very intelligent men bringing forward plans and projects of machines which practically offer no improvement on what has been done, but who, nevertheless, expect to carry anywhere from 160 to 500 lbs. per horse-power expended, while loading their surfaces so that they have to sustain several pounds to each square foot of area.

Theoretically considered 160 lbs. per horse-power seems a reasonably low figure, and with properly regulated apparatus in calm air it may some day be realized.

For the present, however, it seems certain that we must be content with a great deal less, say with 30 to 50 lbs. per horse-power. All the causes which in practice contribute to this great waste of energy are not definitely known, but a few are, and I will endeavor later on to point them out. The chief losses come from imperfect control of the apparatus, disturbances caused by the wind, and the unexpectedly great resistances offered by the framing, wire-guys, and other necessary parts of the apparatus.

It does not take long to evolve a stick and paper model which will glide beautifully and almost without undulation from one end of quite a large room to the other, while not descending more than one foot in every four that it travels. These models may be simple affairs made of writing-paper stiffened with thin spruce sticks or shavings, the whole being afterwards varnished with a thin coat of shellac to preserve the shape. Tried in a closed room their equilibrium seems perfect, but open one of the windows and direct the course of the model across the draught that blows in or out, and it no longer flies well, — in fact, in most cases, it will not fly at all : likewise when tried out-of-doors in even the faintest breeze it becomes a very poor model indeed.

To make a gliding model which will fly well in the open air, and retain its balance and course relatively free from rocking and undulation, requires a considerably better finished piece of apparatus; greater care must be used to get the shape, size, curvature and inclination of the wings exactly alike, — the edges must be sharp, and lastly, the model must be heavier and the centre of gravity be placed farther forward. The slightest variation in any detail often makes all the difference between a very good " flyer " and a very poor one. It will, of course, be observed that these models fly faster, but on the whole they do not fly so far in proportion to the distance they fall, and if the power be computed it will be found that the weight carried per horse-power is less — generally much less.

This weight carried (per horse-power) diminishes rapidly with increase of load, so much so that with one pound per square foot it is a very good model indeed which will indicate the rate of over forty pounds carried per horse-power; this and a little more, however, has been accomplished by several experimenters.

To obtain such a result uniformly, however, in the open air is very difficult; it requires good workmanship and very carefully finished surfaces; these I have generally made upon light frames of spruce, braced and edged with the finest piano wire. The coverings have been of silk or paper coated with shellac; and for very light and strong wings I have used gold-beaters' skin or ox-gut, which, after stretching on the frame, may be drawn as tight as a drum-head, with a couple of coats of pyroxiline varnish. The latter is a form of dissolved celluloid, or more properly a collodion, to which a number of ingredients, such as castor-oil gum, Canada balsam, etc., have been added in small quantities, rendering the film left by the evaporated varnish tough and flexible. This film has a pronounced tendency to shrink. This tendency in a somewhat less degree is communicated to the material to which the varnish is applied.

With even the best of care and workmanship the ordinary models only reach a certain degree of perfection, such that they will keep their equilibrium in a faint wind, say five or six miles an hour; beyond this it seems impossible to go without devising some sort of arrangement for maintaining a uniform angle of advance. The first thing to suggest itself is to use more than one following surface, and perhaps the next is to employ a pendulum directly or indirectly acting upon the rear surface

or upon an auxiliary rudder ; both methods, as well as a combination of the two, are undoubtedly good as makeshifts ; but though
I fell into this error, I am inclined, in the light of more recent developments, to believe that it was a step in the wrong
direction.

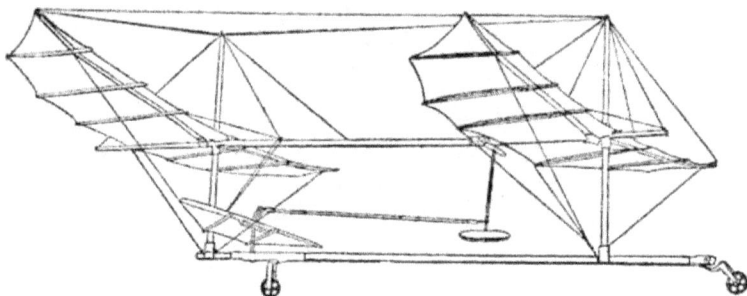

Fig. I.

Figure 1 represents a double wing pendulum model constructed some time ago.   This, when a damper (in the form of
thick grease) was applied to the pendulum axle, seemed to
promise great results.   This model (28 by 28 inches in extreme
dimensions, each pair of wings being 28 by 7 inches) flew
more successfully than anything I had tried before that time.
The fact of its making a number of flights in which the average
travel was five and a half times the fall was the reason of its
being photographed.   The pendulum was afterward replaced
by a gyroscope, which, it is needless to say, failed.   I mention
this model simply because it will give a good illustration of how
hard it often is to definitely locate the exact cause of success or
of failure in this class of experiment.

As the pendulum regulated the small horizontal rudder
(beneath the rear pair of wings) smoothly and gradually for each
and every slight variation from the horizontal position of the
whole apparatus, it was natural to attribute what success there
was to the pendulum and to its connecting mechanism.   Nevertheless it occurred to me to test the matter more definitely;
accordingly the pendulum was tied in several different positions,

and then it was found possible to obtain unmistakably better results than when the pendulum and mechanism were free.

Though I did not appreciate it at the time, I may mention in passing that the chief factors which contributed to the success of the model were, first, the fore and aft position of the centre of gravity (just $1\frac{1}{2}$ in. back of the rear edge of the front wings); second, the vertical position of the centre of gravity, which was by chance so placed that the resistances caused by the wings and framing above were balanced by the resistance of the framing, wheels, etc., below, so that when the model flew at its soaring speed of minimum resistance the efforts were balanced about the centre of gravity.

The expression, " soaring speed of minimum resistance," may not be perfectly clear. If we assume that as the speed increases the model tends to decrease the angle at which the surfaces are presented and thereby to diminish the drift offered by the wings, while at the same time the framing, wires, struts, edges of wings, etc., offer an increasing resistance, it is evident that there must be some speed at which the model will sail on the air while offering the least total resistance.

The velocity thus found, experimentally, is the soaring speed of minimum resistance. In most models it is low, owing to the defective automatic regulation of the angle of advance, and also to the large head resistance offered by the framing, etc.

Although quite a number of steam flying-machines have been constructed, and many of them have been furnished with both light and powerful engines, they have nearly all failed from one or more of three causes: imperfect control of the angle at which the surfaces were presented in flight, improper balancing, or unstable equilibrium.

All three requirements are of the greatest importance; perhaps a complete solution is known for all.

The securing of stable equilibrium is perhaps the hardest problem of all, as the difficulties which it presents are most numerous. If we conceive the wind (and there is never a day that there is not some wind) as a steadily blowing stream of air, — as people generally believe it to be, — a flying-machine

would be a very easy thing to construct, and it would have
been invented long ago. But the air is never wholly at rest,
nor does the wind, as we know, come anywhere near being such
an ideally moving stream of air. According to experiments
made by Zahm and by Wellner, the air, even in the slightest
zephyrs, not only changes the horizontal direction from which it
blows, several times in a second, but it changes in its speed and
in its up and down trend quite as much and quite as rapidly;
not only this, but these relative disturbances are of considerable magnitude, and are more and more pronounced the stronger
the wind. Now, the position of the centre of pressure varies
very much according to the relative inclination of the wind to
the plane, and it also varies with the speed at which the plane
travels. But as the centre of the weight of the machine should
always be under the centre of support (or centre of pressure),
it is easily seen that any changes in the direction or intensity of
the wind will cause a corresponding change in the point of support, and consequently derange the equilibrium of the whole
apparatus; this is not easily reëstablished in an instant.

The best solution is probably to be found in such surfaces,
and their arrangement relative to each other, as will remain
undisturbed by the changes in the wind. This, which has been
the object of very much of my experimental work, for a long

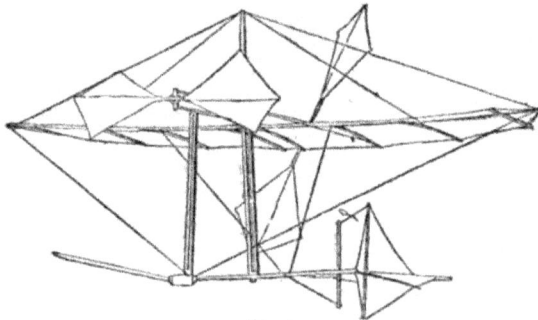

Fig. 2.

time seemed almost a hopeless task, but I believe it has at last
been attained — not perfectly, but nearly so.

In December, 1890, while actively at work on this part of the problem, I constructed a small machine which worked by the power of a twisted rubber spring. The surfaces were in different shapes and arrangements, but finally the model assumed the form shown in the drawings given herewith (Figures 2 and 3). This model, which is still in existence, flies exceedingly well, but it did not do so until the centre of gravity had been properly adjusted beneath the wings and the proper height had been found at which to put the propellers. It is very light, but carries a very great amount of weight in proportion to the power expended. Its flights last from 5 to 7 seconds, during which time it goes from 80 to 135 feet.

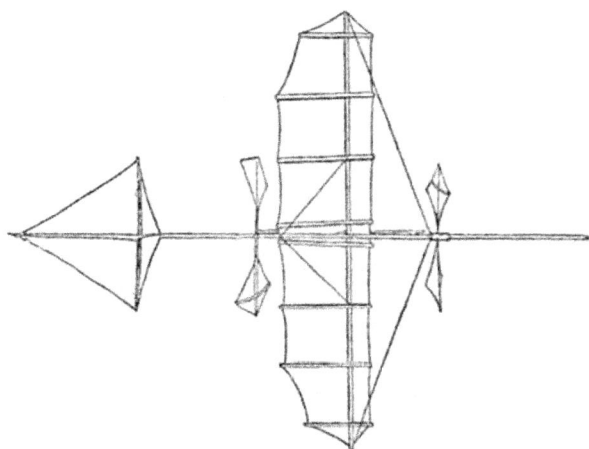

Fig. 3.

To look at the pictures no one would imagine that its conception and construction could have been the work of more than a few days' time at the outside; it represents, nevertheless, the outgrowth of nearly two years' work — one difficulty alone occupying more than four-fifths of the time. I speak of the mechanism which controls its angle of inclination and maintains the model in approximately horizontal flight.

The effect of this regulating mechanism is such as to have decreased the power necessary to propel the model to only one-quarter as much as was necessary without it. A number of trials made in the open air show that it can fly successfully in a wind of over 7 miles an hour. Its velocity is from 12 to 16.3 feet a second with an expenditure of 1.05 to 5 foot-lbs. per second, the former being the least amount it will fly with steadily. The propellers are 16 inches in diameter and make from 11.3 to 24 turns a second per pair. The total weight is 0.30 lbs. and the area of the wings is 258 square inches, or at the rate of 6.0 square feet to the pound; it will, however, fly when loaded with twice its own weight, but requires a greater proportionate expenditure of power.

The model flies well until only about three turns of the spring remain wound. With 15 turns it flies rapidly, while exerting 1.65 foot-lbs. per second.

The slip of the propellers in flight is about 55%, so that at most their efficiency is 45%. This shows that the surfaces carry at the rate of over 200 lbs. (and possibly over 300 lbs.) per " push horse-power." Even the lesser figure is, I believe, considerably higher than has ever been attained by any other free model.

If, however, we were able to bring the rate of loading up to one pound per square foot, instead of one pound to six square feet of surface, we would (theoretically) have to divide the weight carried per horse-power by the square root of six. And if we allow for propellers of 70% efficiency instead of 45%, and also allow for the greater resistance at higher speed, it is probable that instead of carrying 200 to 300 lbs. we could only carry 50 to 60 lbs. per horse-power.

In 1891 I constructed a model similar in design to the above, but provided with a set of compound steam-engines, supplied with an aluminium tubing condenser exposing about nine square feet of surface. The engines, with their pumps, circulator, shafting, boiler, boiler covering, furnace and tanks complete, but not including the condenser, weighed less than one pound, and developed a little over $\frac{2}{10}$ of a horse-power. The condenser, with its joints and connections complete,

weighed only $\frac{85}{100}$ of a pound.   The total weight of the apparatus was five pounds, and the surface was 14 square feet.

The machine succeeded several times in raising itself from
the ground, with its fuel and supplies, and without any outside
aid whatever, even in starting, and I succeeded in getting it to
fly a little over 240 feet.   It sustained a trifle more than 30
pounds per horse-power, and had it not been destroyed by the
explosion of its boiler it is believed that a better adjustment of
the regulator would have enabled the model to carry at the rate
of 50 to 60 pounds per horse-power.

It is a common error to consider the resistances of the framing, guy-wires, edges of wings, etc., as a negligible quantity
where a pound or more per square foot may be economically
carried.   As a matter of fact these resistances, when added together, in some of the very best designs that I have seen, would
consume anywhere from 60% to 500% as much power as allowed
for the aeroplanes (or rather aerocurves).   It is far from correct,
however, to assume that such great resistances are absolutely
unavoidable; yet with very light construction the resistance
offered by the wires alone will always be too great to allow any
machine large enough to carry a man to sail economically at
such small angles and high speeds as have been usually assumed.

Careful experiments lead me to think that 350 feet is, perhaps,
the minimum length of exposed wire which can be used in a
light machine to carry a man; this, at 75 miles an hour, would
offer a head resistance of over 30 pounds, and would consume
over 6 horse-power, nearly 30 times as much power as one man
can exert continuously.

It is, perhaps, safe to say that the resistance of the balance
of the framing, car, etc., would, under the best possible *light*
construction, offer as much as, or more, resistance than the wires
at this speed; and both together would consume a total of over
12 horse-power in friction, and yet there are hundreds of
well-informed people who believe that if they could regulate
their apparatus they would be able to fly 100 miles an hour or
more by their own exertion!

As we cannot at present regulate our apparatus with any

very great degree of certainty, we cannot sail at small angles; we cannot therefore carry very much per horse-power, and are necessarily limited to lightly-built machines; these, of course, must be braced with almost an innumerable number of small wires to make them sufficiently strong and stiff.

Notwithstanding the great resistance which such a construction offers, it is the best for speed of less than 35 miles an hour, and this is, perhaps, above the speed that will be attained by the first machine that successfully carries (by power) a man in the air.

Perhaps the subject on which there are the least reliable data is the law governing the position of the centre of pressure under the varying conditions of inclination and speed; yet in the design of any model or large apparatus it is probably of more importance than any other single item.

If in a close room the model shown in Figure 1 be launched from the hand, it may be found by repeated trial that the centre of pressure of the combined surfaces can travel so far forward as to come beneath the front wings, instead of remaining about one-third way between the two pair; yet it is apparently not in the same place when the model is flown parallel to and near the floor, as when it is thrown off from about 6 or 7 feet above it. Also, the centre of pressure is apparently farther forward at high velocities than at low, and when the model is balanced for rapid flight it will not sail satisfactorily at slow speed. Similarly a light model made for gliding flight, and consequently for slow speed, is wholly unfit for rapid flight.

The lifting power of planes set at various angles and driven at various speeds seems to be well determined, thanks to the labors of Professor Langley. Concerning curved surfaces, which are far more efficient, there is not so much reliable information.

One very noticeable difference is shown between experiments made in the natural wind and those which are made with a " whirling table " where the surface is driven against an artificial wind produced by motion through still air.

The difference is very largely in favor of the natural wind, which, roughly speaking, gives an average effect very much greater than that produced by moving the same surface through apparently still air.

I have found that in experimenting with small surfaces it is not entirely correct to apply the data thus obtained directly, to similar but very much larger surfaces.

I found a difference in the resistance and lifting power of large surfaces compared with small ones. The larger are generally more efficient. At the same speed they lift more per square foot, and apparently offer slightly less resistance or drift per pound lifted; the centre of pressure is also proportionately slightly farther back.

I have further found that a most striking relation exists between the maximum travel of the centre of pressure of surfaces and the efficiency of those surfaces when compared to some standard (such as a plane).

In general, the less the maximum departure of the centre of pressure from the centre of figure, the greater is the efficiency of the surface, and the greater is the amount which it will lift at a given angle with a given speed; and also the greater is the weight which can be carried by the expenditure of one horse-power.

At almost all angles of inclination the centre of pressure on a square plane is proportionately farther forward than is the centre of pressure on a plane whose advancing edge is five times its breadth. Similarly, at slight angles, the centre of pressure on a properly curved surface (whose vertical projection is square) is farther back than either.

Another variation in the position of the centre of pressure is that produced by speed. If a plane or slightly curved surface be held in a wind and be inclined at a very flat angle, its centre of pressure will be found farther forward at high speed than at low.

The centre of pressure on considerably curved surfaces undergoes a peculiar reversal in its position. In one in which the curvature is such that the rise of arc is about ⅛ the chord length, and where the highest point of curvature is ⅓ the way from the front, the maximum forward position of the centre of pressure is found when the surface is tilted at about five degrees; it, however, travels rapidly backward for either a lesser or a greater inclination of the chord.

This peculiar reversal is probably due to the air pressure on the upper side of the front margin, and does not necessarily mean that such a surface is more efficient at an inclination of 1 or 2 degrees than it is at 5 degrees.

The maximum forward position of the centre of pressure in such a surface is about 37 to 39 per cent. of its width; this places it very high in point of efficiency.

In 1894 I built three gliding-machines. The object in the construction of these was twofold: first, to learn, if possible, what the difficulties would be in the management of the machine in the air; and, second, to find approximately the power required to sustain a man and a machine in flight.

The difficulties encountered in gliding flight are almost entirely confined to those introduced by the irregularities of the wind; at least such is the case when you have once learnt how to start; this, perhaps, is the most difficult point of all to master in the beginning, as it is necessary to get up a very considerable speed while running down a fairly steep incline, the speed is so great, — 18 to 20 miles an hour in a calm, — that you invariably feel safer on the machine in the air than you do during the preliminary run.

In trials in a fairly brisk wind, the direction from which the latter blows varies very considerably and irregularly, so much so that the muscular exertion required in shifting the weight so as to always correspond with the centre of pressure on the wings is very great.

The shifting of the latter in the line of flight appears not only to depend on the angle at which the machine is tilted, but also upon the velocity of the air relative to the machine.

At the same inclination the centre of pressure is farther forward at high speed than at low speed, and reaches its maximum forward position in the frequent gusts which one is liable to encounter in flight.

The fore and aft travel is also very great for even small

changes in the inclination of the apparatus. This is not so difficult to counteract as is the disturbance produced by variations in the amount of upward and downward trend of the wind; this comes suddenly and unexpectedly, as does also the lateral variation, which causes one wing or the other to lift the more. The last-mentioned difficulty, is, perhaps, the worst of all; it is very great with wings which are long and narrow, but, I believe, it has been very largely overcome by the discovery of a highly efficient surface which possesses the remarkable quality of having little or no travel to its centre of pressure from front to back, and which, furthermore, is almost equally efficient in square shape as when the length is very much greater than the depth. This surface will lift its own weight in a light breeze when the chord of the surface is inclined at so great a negative angle as 15 to 20 degrees.

When properly loaded a model made with this surface was found to glide quite a distance at surprisingly low speed.

Many of the foremost workers on the flying-machine problem are firm believers in the possibility of man learning to soar by utilizing the forces of the wind, as the birds do, but for my own part, if this be ever accomplished, I believe it will be long after the air has been navigated by steam. This, in spite of the difficulties which a few years ago seemed unsurmountable, is not only a probability but is apparently a certainty of the near future. Progress in the " new science " has been very rapid within the past three years, and many of the most formidable barriers to success have disappeared. Much of this advance is due to one man, Mr. Chanute, of Chicago, whose thorough knowledge of the subject and whose acute powers of analysis have been of incalculable benefit to several experimenters, and to myself in particular.

THE REVOLVING SLOPE.

NEW ideas are constantly coming to the mind of Mr. Albert A. Merrill, the secretary of the Boston Aeronautical Society. It was he who originally proposed the formation of the Society, and who awakened the interest of the first members by calling upon them. The accompanying drawing shows one of his inventions.

The object is to provide a suitable slope for the starting of any aerial machine. It is desirable to start all flights when facing the wind, as is the habit of all the larger birds. Mr. Lilienthal has usually started from the summit of a hill. In his earlier experiments, the hill which he used did not have the desired slope in all directions; consequently he suffered long delays while the wind held in unfavorable quarters. So he has had a conical hill built which slopes toward all points of the compass, and whenever any wind is blowing he can face it.

Mr. Merrill thinks that artificial hills will be too expensive for common use, and in order to accomplish the desired result more economically and more conveniently he has invented the Revolving Slope.

As indicated in the drawing, this is a building moving upon a pivot, P, and turning upon a circular track similar to that of a locomotive turn-table. The slope can thus be made to face the wind from any quarter. The building serves as a work-shop and as a place for the storage of the flying apparatus. When a higher point of starting is needed, for instance, one hundred feet or more, the Revolving Slope can be made of steel trestle-work, which, being open, will not be injured by storms.

Mr. Merrill writes: " For the first structure I would select a large and level plot of soft ground (by soft, I mean free from rocks), within, say, a dozen miles or so of a city, and in a windy locality.

" In the centre of this I would build my workshop, of which the side and end elevations are given. It is seen by the plan that I have made my workshop take the place of Lilienthal's hill. The building is 60 ft. × 12 ft. on the base, by 24 ft. high. It has a flat roof 12 ft. × 12 ft., and the rest of the 60-ft. base is covered by a pitched roof. This roof covers the

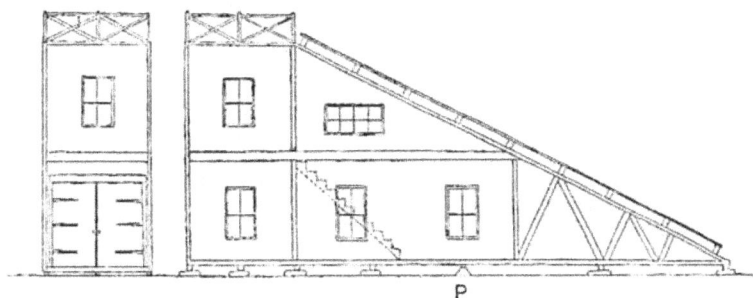

P

entire width of the building. Thirty-six feet of the base of the building are enclosed in walls of matched boards, making a lower room of 36 ft. × 12 ft. × 12 ft., with an upper room 36 ft. × 12 ft. × 12 ft., having a slanting roof. These rooms receive light from the windows as represented, and entrance is effected by the large doors shown in the left-hand view.

" With such a space there would be abundant room for work-bench, tools, models, etc., while the attic could be used for other purposes. In this way the building would be complete in itself, and all kinds of experimental work could go on in its interior, while its roof could be used to test perfected apparatus. The pivot upon which the building turns is seen in the drawing under the right-hand window; and although this is the turning-point, most of the weight is carried by the heavy wooden rollers under the joist, as seen in the plans. The building is turned by a windlass inside; its weight, about five tons, while enough to make it stand firmly, will not interfere

with its movement around the pivot. I would advise having
steel cables running from the roof to the ground, on each side,
to steady the structure, and I think it a good plan to have it
built in sections to facilitate transportation. There are many
details which perhaps can be worked out by others much better
than by myself, and in concluding I can only say that when,
some months ago, I suggested this to a body of scientific men,
I was assured of the plan being practical by a successful car-
penter and builder to whom I went for advice, and who not
only believes it possible to carry out the above, but who has
now such plans and specifications in his possession as warrant
him in saying that the building could be constructed in his
shop, transported to the field, and set up in good condition for
about $500.

" It seems to me that with the use of such a building great
progress would be made in aerial navigation, at slight expense
to the investigators."

THE RELATION OF THE WIND TO AERONAUTICS.

By A. Lawrence Rotch,

Director of Blue Hill Meteorological Observatory.

It is obvious that a knowledge of the velocity and direction of the air currents which may be encountered at moderate elevations above the earth is of great importance to experimenters in aeronautics.

The situation of the Blue Hill Observatory, about 500 feet above the general level of the country around Boston, with a free exposure in all directions, makes the data relating to the wind collected there very valuable, and therefore special attention has been given to such investigations since the establishment of the Observatory in 1885.

Mean Velocity of the Wind at Different Altitudes. — It is well known that there is an increase of wind as we rise above the ground, on account of the retardation caused by the irregularities of the earth's surface. Thus the anemometer on the Blue Hill Observatory records on the average about 60 per cent. more wind than does the instrument on the Boston Post-Office tower, 460 feet lower, but still nearly 200 feet above the city streets. During the past few months kites have been used to extend the range of observation 2,000 feet above Blue Hill, where, by means of a series of especially designed kites, a meteorograph constructed by Mr. S. P. Fergusson, of the Observatory, recorded automatically the temperature and wind velocity at intermediate heights, which were determined by trigonometrical measurements. Excepting certain abnormal cases when the wind decreased aloft, the velocity increased about 25 per cent. at an elevation of from 1,000 to 2,000 feet above the hill. There is, however, reason for believing that slightly above the hill the wind velocity is less, or at least no greater, than on the Observatory tower, the hill acting as an obstacle to the air stream which then flows over it with accelerated speed, like water over a dam. This is certainly the case on Mount Washington, where the observed wind has a greater velocity than have the clouds at the same level.

Since a free balloon takes the motion of the air in which it floats, it is an excellent anemometer, and by noting the times of starting and landing and the places passed over, the velocity and direction of the wind at the average level of the balloon are obtained. This was done by the writer in two ascents from Paris, which serve to confirm the recent kite experiments. In the first voyage, at an average height of about 2,000 feet, the balloon was carried at the rate of 22 miles an hour, while during the same time on the Eiffel Tower, at half that altitude, the wind blew 18 miles an hour. In the second voyage, with an average height of 2,900 feet, the balloon moved 20 miles an hour, while on the Eiffel Tower, 1,900 feet lower, the wind was only 16 miles.

The trigonometrical cloud measurements which were made at the Blue Hill Observatory during 1890 and 1891, by Messrs. Clayton and Fergusson, enable the velocity and direction of the currents carrying clouds at different levels to be calculated. Above the hill the increase of velocity with altitude is regular and uniform, winter and summer, up to the cirrus clouds at an elevation of 8 miles, whose summer velocity averages 79 miles per hour. Starting with a mean summer velocity of 15.3 miles per hour at the top of the hill, the increase in miles per hour for each 330 feet of elevation at various levels up to the greatest height likely to be reached by dirigible and self-propelled aeroplanes is given in the table on page 107.

The slight decrease in velocity between 3,300 and 5,200 feet is probably caused by the slower-moving currents ascending from a lower level, by which the cumulus clouds at that level are formed. The mean of all the increments gives a mean rate of increase of 0.64 mile per hour per 330 feet, the increase in winter being 1.45 miles, or more than twice as rapid.

Height in feet.	1,300 to 2,000	2,000 to 2,600	2,600 to 3,300	3,300 to 3,900	3,900 to 4,600	4,600 to 5,200	5,200 to 5,900	5,900 to 6,600
Increase per 330 ft.	+2.2	+1.6	+2.0	−1.6	−0.2	−0.2	+1.1	+0.7

Height in feet.	6,600 to 7,200	7,200 to 8,200	8,200 to 9,300	9,300 to 10,800
Increase per 330 ft.	+0.2	+1.1	+0.2	+0.9

Maximum Wind Velocity and Pressure. — The greatest velocity or pressure which aeroplanes may encounter is necessary of consideration in order that the motive power may be sufficient to make headway, or at least that the parts may be strong enough to resist the pressure to which they may be subjected.

A balloon moving with the wind experiences but slight resistance, whereas a self-propelled apparatus which might be capable of travelling 10 miles per hour in still air would remain stationary, as regards the earth, when it encountered a contrary wind of 10 miles per hour, and yet there would be actually blowing against it the wind of 10 miles per hour, whose pressure was nearly half a pound upon each square foot of surface normally exposed. If the machine could travel 20 miles per hour and the natural wind blew at half this rate against it, the machine would advance at the rate of 10 miles and would sustain a pressure of about one and a half pounds per square foot, the pressure increasing as the square of the velocity of the impinging air. This factor seems to impose practical limits to the use of air ships against high winds.

The mean velocity of the wind on Blue Hill is about 15 miles per hour in summer and 22 miles in winter, and these may be

taken to represent the usual velocities 400 or 500 feet above
this part of the country.   An extreme velocity of 88 miles per
hour during five minutes has been recorded, which, according
to the mean of the best formulæ for converting velocity into
pressure of normal surface ($P = v^2 \times .0035$) gives a pressure of
28 lbs. per square foot.   During the first four years of observation a self-recording pressure-plate was in operation, and on two
occasions pressures of over 43 lbs. on the square foot were registered, while the corresponding velocity during five minutes was
only 85 miles per hour instead of 110 miles, as the pressure
would indicate.   This seemed to show that the extreme pressures are of very short duration, perhaps lasting only a few
seconds, and the supposition was confirmed by an elaborate
series of comparisons of different types of anemometers which
has just been completed by Mr. Fergusson.   The use of anemometers and pressure-plates recording at short intervals, with
large time scales, shows that the wind is exceedingly variable,
and that the frequency and intensity of gusts is generally greatest at high velocities.   Usually, in a brisk wind, sudden blows or
jerks followed by intervals of very slight pressure will succeed
each other with great rapidity, often several times a second.   It
is now demonstrated that the cups of the Robinson anemometer
(which is the instrument in general use) do not move one-
third as fast as the wind, and that the factor for the pattern used
by our Weather Bureau is, at moderate velocities, 2.65 instead
of 3.   Applying this correction, a recorded velocity of 30 miles
per hour is reduced to 26, but recorded velocities below 6 miles
per hour require to be slightly increased.

The maximum velocities of clouds at different levels which
have been measured at Blue Hill, by the method already mentioned, are as follows:

Height in feet .	. 1,660	5,300	12,650	21,750	29,130
Velocity in miles per hour,	40	69	74	150	230

Inclination and Direction of the Wind. — It is generally assumed that the wind blows horizontally, and our ordinary anemometers measure only the horizontal component. Of late years

an instrument for recording the vertical component has been in use at Zi-Ka-Wei, China, and on the Eiffel Tower in Paris, which showed the existence of both upward and downward currents. In 1891 such an instrument was exposed 30 feet above the tower of the Blue Hill Observatory, and observations were made during several months. Upward currents aggregating one thousand feet per day were recorded, due chiefly to the deflection of the horizontal wind on striking the hill, since the vertical wind was roughly proportional to the amount of horizontal wind, but it was also related to the heating of the hill by the sun, being strongest in clear weather. Downward currents were seldom registered, proving that, though they undoubtedly exist, their velocity was too small to affect the fans of the anemometer. That these vertical currents may extend to considerable heights is shown by the production of cumulus clouds, under which the kites have demonstrated the existence of strong ascensional currents. The wave-like appearance of the higher clouds is also evidence of undulatory movements which may extend downwards to the earth, and cause rhythmical oscillations of the barometer. We are not yet prepared to say to what extent these upward currents may be utilized to lift aeroplanes, and the theory that the soaring bird is always sustained by them has not yet been generally accepted.

The wind direction at different levels is important for the aeronaut, and here again the cloud observations at Blue Hill and their discussion by Mr. Clayton have contributed much data. The cyclonic and anticyclonic circulations which control our surface winds are entirely masked above the cumulus region — that is, above the height of a mile — by the general drift from the west-northwest, which deflects the currents to the right in the cyclones and to the left in the anticyclones. Mr. Clayton found that the currents do not all turn to the right as one ascends into the atmosphere, as is usually stated. When the winds have a southerly component, the upper currents come from a direction more and more to the right as one ascends, but when the winds have a northerly component the currents turn to the left as one ascends. In the two balloon voyages already mentioned, the upper winds veered with respect to the lower; that is, they were deflected towards the right hand, and this was the case from the earth's surface up. On these days the surface winds were southerly, and the general circulation was controlled by an area of high barometric pressure in the west.

Diurnal Changes of Velocity and Direction. — If navigating the air ever becomes practicable, the hourly variations of the wind will doubtless have to be considered. There are generally two daily maxima and two daily minima of wind velocity. The chief maximum occurs on Blue Hill during the afternoon, and the chief minimum in the early morning, the hours varying with the seasons. The difference between the chief maximum and chief minimum for the year at Blue Hill is 1.8 miles per hour, but at Boston, nearer sea level, it is 3.3 miles, or more than one-fourth of the mean velocity. In the open sea the diurnal change is very small, but as we rise in the air the time of minimum velocity shifts towards noon, so that on Pike's Peak the low-level conditions are almost completely reversed, the greatest velocity here occurring early in the morning and the least at noon. This appears due to the fact that ascending currents begin near the earth's surface in the early morning and gradually extend higher and higher until the afternoon. The first effect of the ascending air is to retard the more rapidly moving air into which it enters, but as it ascends higher and the more rapidly moving air descends to supply its place, the currents beneath are again accelerated. It therefore results that at low levels the night winds have not only a less average velocity than the day winds, but they are more steady, for the reason that they are not affected by local rising convectional currents. The night, consequently, is the most suitable time to experiment with most aeronautical apparatus.

The diurnal change of wind direction is not so well marked as the change in velocity, but there has been found at Blue Hill and elsewhere a tendency of the wind at all heights to veer around the compass each day. This is independent of the sea breeze, which affects only the surface winds.

THE KITE CONSIDERED AS AN INSTRUMENT OF VALUE.

By the Editor.

THERE are many reasons for thinking that in the development of the kite we have a study from which useful knowledge may be gained. The equipment necessary for kite-designing and kite-flying being comparatively inexpensive, these occupations are open to many who like to combine open-air exercise with study. Perhaps it can be shown that the kite is worthy of more attention than it has hitherto received.

Three forces act upon a flying kite: (1) the wind, (2) gravity, (3) the string. The pull upon a kite-string is the resultant of two components: (1) lift, (2) drift.[1] It is evident that when a kite is well designed the string may be relieved of a part of the pull which is caused by component number one, the lift. This may be done by making the kite a weight-carrier. It being desirable in the extreme to increase the efficiency of the kite as a weight-carrier, our greatest efforts in designing should be to

---

[1] These technical terms are in common use in the discussions of aeronautical matters. Sir George Cayley wrote of these forces in 1809. (See Aero. Annual, 1895, p. 20.) Mentioning the whole force of the air under the wing of the horizontally soaring bird, he says that it may be resolved into two forces, one representing the force that sustains the weight of the bird, the other the retarding force by which the velocity of its motion is constantly diminished. Sir George seems to have been the first student of aeronautics to understand these forces. He applied no names to them. Later writers have used the word *lift* to designate the former and *drift* the latter. Maxim uses the words as follows, in describing a piece of apparatus which he has designed for experiments to ascertain the best possible fabric to be used for sustaining surfaces. He says: " It is constructed in such a manner that a piece of the fabric to be tested can be tightly stretched on a small steel frame, and mounted at an angle in a blast of air, with suitable weighing-apparatus for ascertaining the lift and the drift — 'drift' in this sense meaning the tendency of the object to move in the direction of the wind, while ' lift ' means its ascensional force."

The fitness of the chosen words will be seen when they are applied to the kite; *lift* being the weight-carrying power and *drift* the tendency to move to leeward.

obtain the maximum of lift with the minimum of drift, thus bringing the kite nearer to the zenith and decreasing the size and weight of the string which is necessary to control it.

By experiments at York, Me., during the past summer I have tried to learn:

1st.   What forms of kite fly with the greatest steadiness.

2d.   What is the best way to make the kite a weight-carrier.

In my efforts to secure steadiness of flight I have experimented with kites of many different types, some of which are shown by the drawings on these pages. My first experiments were made with single kites. Fig. 1 shows a Chinese kite.

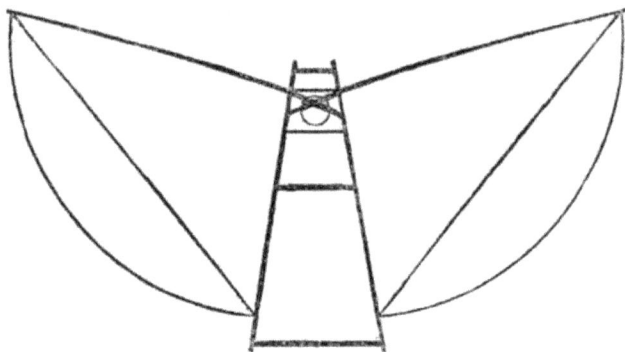

Fig. 1. — Single Chinese Kite. The segments of circles are loose flaps.

This was copied from one of a large collection which formed a part of the Chinese exhibit at the Centennial Exhibition in Philadelphia.

Having tried this and various other forms of single kite without getting just the results looked for, I was led to make experiments to ascertain to what extent longitudinal stability [1] may be improved by an increase of the long dimension. The results were, on the whole, satisfactory.

Early in the season I visited Mr. C. H. Lamson, of Portland, Me., and I found that he had obtained a decided increase of

---

[1] The word *stability* is here used to designate steadiness of flight. When firmness of structure is meant, the word *rigidity* will be used.

stability by doubling his kite, *i.e.*, by putting two single Malay kites upon one backbone. Acting upon his suggestion, I doubled my Chinese kite as shown in Fig. 2, and it has

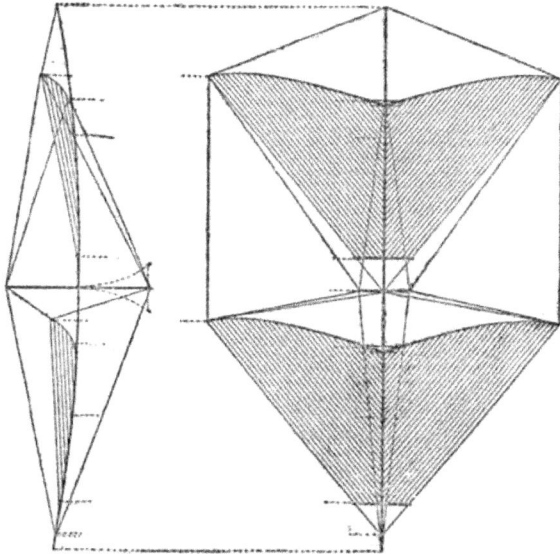

Fig. 2.

proved to be much superior to the single form. It flies at a good angle, all things considered, and, under favorable conditions, with great steadiness. I have seen it maintain its equilibrium in a high wind until its material yielded and it went to tatters.

It will be noticed in Fig. 1 that the single Chinese kite is made with loose flaps. Wishing to ascertain what effect, if any, these had upon the stability of the kite, I had the double Chinese made with the flaps, and one day when the kite was at its best in a strong wind, I lowered it and cut off the flaps. When the kite was immediately raised again, no difference in its flight was perceptible. Every kite-flyer knows that some kites which seem to have stability in ordinary winds are thrown out of equilibrium when the wind strengthens to a certain extent.

My search has been for the steadiest form possible, consequently I have tried everything that time has permitted.

Remarks on page 257 of Mr. Chanute's book[1] led me to have a keel kite constructed. This was tried many times under conditions presumably favorable, yet in every trial it dove to the ground. The keel was placed under the kite something like a boat's keel. The success of Mr. Lamson with another form of keel kite seems to show that my keel was not well placed.

In various lines of experiment it is found that the importance of a principle may be tested by carrying the application of it to an extreme. Therefore, in order to see the effect of further increase in the long dimension, I had a sextuple kite made as shown in Fig. 3. This seemed to be not so good as the double

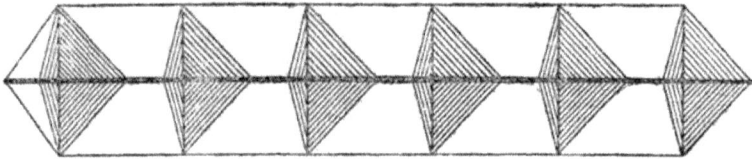

Fig. 3.

kite. I should state, however, that I have not yet tested the sextuple under many different conditions.

I then had a light triple kite made, about twelve feet long. This was on the general plan of Mr. Lamson's kite, only it had three surfaces instead of two. This proved to be so stable and seemed to adapt itself so readily to unfavorable conditions, such as gusts and eddies, that I immediately made drawings for a larger one of the same proportions and about eighteen feet long. When this kite was finished, its flight was fairly satisfactory.

At this stage of the experiments I began to encounter the difficulty of making things hold together. The first triple kite had broken its backbone two or three times, and in flying this large triple in a strong breeze on the 19th of August, and standing a little to leeward of it when its altitude was low, I noticed

---

[1] "Progress in Flying Machines," M. N. Forney, 47 Cedar street, N.Y., 1894.

that the irregularities of its flight were caused by distortion under wind pressure. The next day the kite was flown again in a stronger wind, and the backbone broke near the centre.

The following day the kite was repaired and flown again. When 3,166 feet of string were out, the line parted. What became of the kite I have not learned. Boone Island is six miles from shore and ten miles from where the kite left the ground; fishermen near this island last saw the kite and reported it as very high in the air and rapidly travelling seaward. Measurement upon the reel showed that the kite had carried away about 1,400 feet of string, and, as a well-balanced kite with a drag-line of just the right length — as this seemed to be — is self-regulating, I think the kite must have travelled until it came to a calm spot.

I then made drawings for another triple, which was soon completed. The dimensions [1] are the same as those of its predecessor, but, unlike that, it is a very strong kite for its weight of six pounds, the backbone being trussed with steel wire, and it is still in good condition for use next summer. All of the details are given in the explanation of Plate XII. I have seen this kite fly with great steadiness in a strong wind, and I can recommend it as a useful one for the beginner.

The foregoing refers to efforts made to secure steadiness of flight. The second division of the subject relates to the carrying of weights. In the kite-designing of the future this query will often arise when new designs are unsuccessful: *Is a very small factor of drift compatible with the preservation of stability ?*

If future experiments give an unmistakable negative answer to this, then the kite may remain of no more importance than it has been; yet I see now no reason to suppose that the answer will be a negative one.

The curves of the surfaces of the kite must be modified and brought more into conformity with the Lilienthal and the Maxim curves, treated of in other articles. The disposition of the surfaces is a most interesting subject, and calls for a series of experiments as endless as the designing of marine vessels.

---

[1] See footnote on p. 116 for dimensions.

From what has already been said it will be seen that as kite-designing progresses, designers will not be satisfied with mere stability, but, always taking pains to retain those elements which they find conducive to stability, they will endeavor to increase the lift and to lessen the drift.

Unfavorable conditions of wind near the ground often make it difficult to start weighted kites.   If a swivel and pulley block are attached as shown in Fig. 4, and if a double line running through the block be used to fly the kite in lieu of a single line, different weights may be raised to the kite, and after their effect has been ascertained they may be lowered.

The season came to an end before I was able to complete my experiments to determine the weight-carrying power of the triple kite.   I hope to make a later report concerning that matter.

The uses of the kite will now be briefly considered.   It has been maintained by some experimenters in aeronautics that the

---

Explanation of Plate XII.   Triple Malay Kite, 1895.

Spruce frame.   Backbone FL is curved as shown in the upper figure.   MN, OP, etc., are spruce uprights $\frac{1}{2}$ in. $\times$ $\frac{3}{4}$ in. and 12 to 20 inches in length, according to position.   MO, etc., NP, etc., and also the diagonal lines, are taut steel wires.   Backbone is 18 ft. long, $\frac{1}{2}$ in. thick, $1\frac{1}{4}$ in. wide in the centre, tapering to $\frac{7}{8}$ in. wide at the ends. From L to A measured on the stick 1 ft. 6 in.   From A to K, 9 in.   From K to B, 3 ft. 9 in.   From B to C, from D to E, 18 in. each.   GH, QR, and ST are bows each 5 ft. long before bending.   They are $\frac{1}{2}$ in. $\times$ $\frac{3}{4}$ in.   When bows are bent the bow-strings in their centres are about 5 inches from the wood.   (See article on the Eddy Kite in Editorial Department.)   The surfaces BGAH, DQCR, and FSET are equal.

The curves of the backbone and the three cross-bows have their convex sides toward the wind.   This kite is covered with very strong Manila paper.   Weight of the whole kite, 6 lbs.   Textile fabric made impervious to air and moisture would make a better covering.   SR, TQ, QH, RG, SQGL, TRHL, are taut steel-wire stays. The kite is bridled as follows: Find a point on the backbone between D and E 4 inches from D, here attach two cords, each 2 or 3 feet long, drop them so that one will be on one side and the other on the opposite side of the wire NP, unite the ends of the two cords, and rig a chafing-gear on the wire NP so that the cords may not be cut.   Attach a long single cord to the cords just united.   Pull taut and measure off 16 feet 3 inches from the point of attachment between D and E.   Call this point on the cord W.   Let the cord fall in a bight and secure W to the backbone at A.   Now take four or five galvanized-iron rings and fasten them by marline to the cord, the first one about 7 ft. 4 inches from A, the next about 7 ft. 7 in., and so on at intervals of 3 inches.   At the end of the line from the reel place a small snap-hook.   When this is snapped into the ring 7 ft. 10 inches from A, the remainder of the bridle measuring 8 ft. 5 in., the kite will be bridled as when last flown.   Still, no two kites are alike, and it may be that better results will be obtained from a new kite if the snap-hook is fastened to one of the other rings.   Be particular to preserve the symmetry in framing and covering, or your labor will be wasted.

Plate XII.

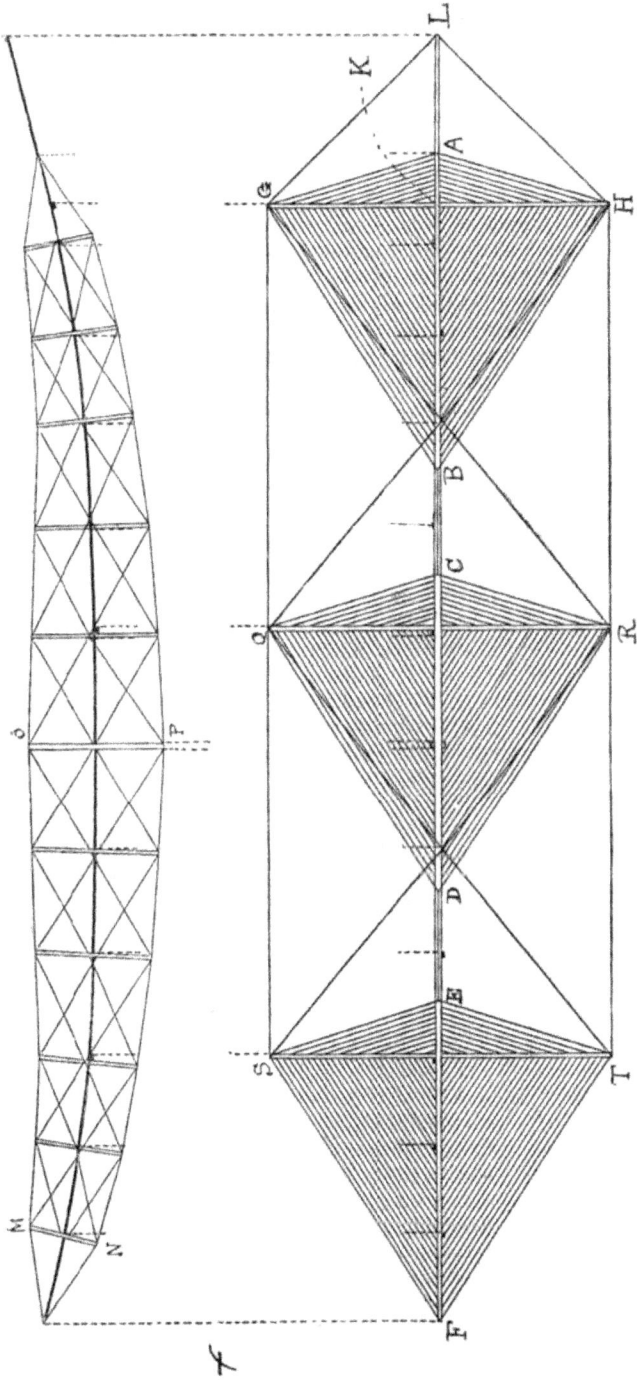

TRIPLE MALAY KITE. 1895.

Intentionally blank as was the original edition.

successful aerial machine of the future will be so designed that
it may be raised in the air as a kite and while remaining
anchored will act as one.   It seems to me that the development of the kite must progress further before the correctness
or incorrectness of this view can be determined, for we do not
yet know the possibilities of the kite.

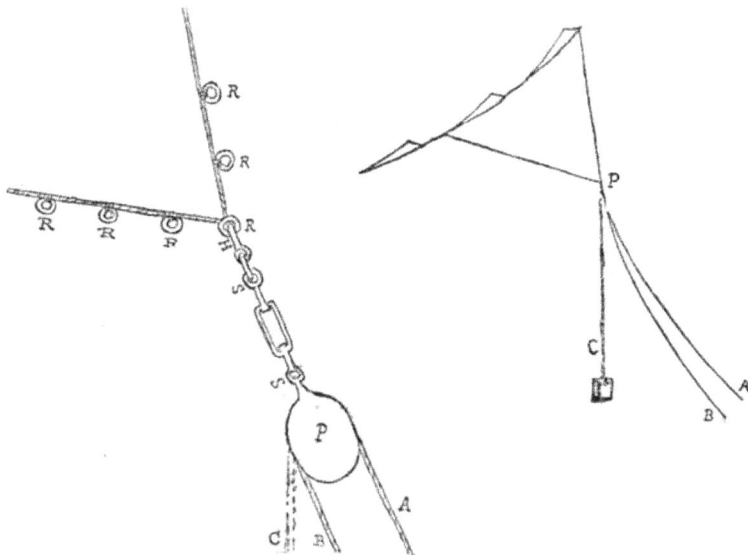

Fig. 4. — H, a snap-hook attachable to any of the rings RRR. SS, a swivel. P, a pulley-block.
The kite is raised by the line APB; then weights are attached to B, which is slowly released,
the weight swinging free, as shown by the dotted line at C. The weight rises to the kite.
Under some conditions it may be necessary to steady the weight by a small guy-line.

It is presumable that the flying-machines of the future will
be of various types and various speeds.   When we consider
the low average velocity of the wind, we are led to think that
only low-speed machines will act as kites in ordinary winds.
Even if this be so, the practices of kite-designing and kite-
flying seem likely to give us useful knowledge.

Mr. A. Lawrence Rotch, the founder of the Blue Hill
Meteorological Observatory, shows in another article the great
value which kites may have in his line of research.

Still another advantage which may come from the practice of kite-making should be carefully noted. In constructing large kites the difficulties of securing the requisite strength, rigidity, and lightness of framing are precisely the difficulties which, among others, are to confront the designers of flying-machines. Hence it is quite evident that kite men are in a position to give direct aid to flying-machine men by their tests of materials for surfaces, frames, and stays, and of the various methods of light and strong construction.

It is hoped that experimenters, young and old, will be led to compete for the prizes mentioned on another page.[1]

---

[1] See article entitled *The Boston Aeronautical Society's Experiment Fund.*

THE MALAY KITE.

By J. B. Millet.

INTEREST in kite-flying, born a few years ago, grows apace. The printed accounts of elevations reached, or pounds lifted, or wind velocities successfully combated, with comparatively fragile structures, excite the ambitions of many who have formerly looked upon a kite as a child's toy; and with the increasing competition we are sure to get results of great value. Such results will quite as likely be reached by the novice as by the more experienced, provided the former is contented to begin where others have left off in devising a form of kite, rather than pin his faith upon some theoretical structure constructed in an imagination thawed by an open fire on a winter evening. It is this very fact — that the novice may be the more successful kite-flyer — that makes the sport unusually attractive. Once into it he finds it to be a constant fight with the wind, opposing light and fragile forms to wind pressures which are apparently vastly out of proportion. Frequent breakages, inexplicable contortions in the air, eccentric misbehavior under what appear to be the most favorable conditions, all draw heavily upon patience, without which quality in abundance the kite-flyer cannot exist.

After spending a whole day in constructing a tailless kite it is certainly discouraging to see it wrecked in the first strong puff, or dashed to the ground through some mistake in hanging or balance, concerning which there have been until very recently almost no data within reach. Even to-day, after all that has been written on kites within the last two or three years, I should not know where to turn to find, for example, satisfactory answers to these questions:

1.   Why does a kite fly without a tail, like the Malay, and what are the best proportions and materials?

2.   Why does a Malay kite dart and dive to the ground, and why does it sag slowly to the ground on one side or the other?

3.   Where on the hanger is the proper point to tie on the guy line?

These problems present themselves early in the day, and can only be answered by experience. Theories, in my opinion, seldom "work out" in kite-flying: it is always a question of "try it and see."

Certain facts, however, are now well established by the experience of the many who fly kites, and the purpose of this paper is to set forth some of these facts in order to aid those who wish to make experiments of their own.   I expressly disclaim any pretence of being able to solve many of the problems that may arise.   An experience of four years has developed a degree of humility in the presence of a well-behaved kite that forbids me to be too sure of anything.   There are, however, facts enough relating to structure and probable behavior to give the beginner an excellent start.

To return, therefore, to the three questions above.   The Malay, or tailless, kite is selected because it is the best form of flat single plane kite at the present time.   There are other tailless forms, but none have been sufficiently tested, and all are in one way or another a deviation from the Malay plan. These deviations waste more time than they are worth, unless the inventor has spent a great deal of time on Malay kites ; and beginners are especially cautioned not to waste time and effort on any self-invented or just-heard-of plan, until they have tried a few Malays, and learned from them about what to expect in varying conditions of wind.   The beginner not only learns what a kite is, but he gets ideas about the action of the wind, the currents which are affected by the continuity of the land, the position of hills, trees, etc., etc.   He will soon realize that the Malay kite is the primer spelling-book and fourth reader in the school of kites.   Fortunately its construction is easy, for exact proportions may be had, and if built with ordinary care it flies at once with a degree of success that is almost always improved upon by subsequent trials.

For ordinary use in gentle winds (from four to ten miles an hour), the following measurements will be found trustworthy:

The cross-stick AB in the accompanying drawing is bent back (before being tied on the upright at E) until the chord of the arc (in other words, the string to the bow) is 10% shorter than the stick AB. This gives the diedral angle to the kite, which is the first factor in establishing the balance without the use of a tail. The sticks are of straight spruce 5 ft. by $\frac{3}{4}$ in. by $\frac{5}{8}$, or even $\frac{1}{2}$ by $\frac{1}{4}$ for very light winds, up to, say, eight miles. Such kites as these do most excellent work if covered with manila paper of light weight, although I always use thin bond-paper, which is very strong even when damp.

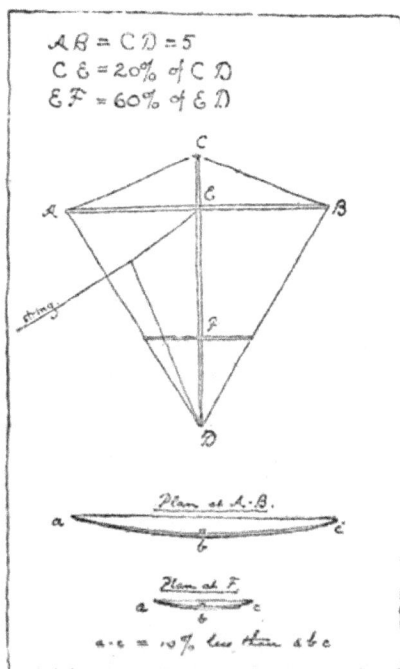

Millet's Modified Malay Kite.

For winds from ten miles up to thirty or thirty-five, the kite must be smaller and the sticks stronger, and the cover cloth instead of paper. Personally I have found that a four-foot kite or a four and a half foot at the outside, is plenty large enough. Kites of this grade must be made much stiffer and of more durable material. The sticks are 4 ft. by $\frac{1}{2}$ by $\frac{3}{4}$, and the covering should be of cloth — any light cloth that is not porous and will not stretch much. Percaline or light cotton-cloth are the best among the inexpensive materials, and so far as my experience goes they give quite as good results as silk. The great advantage in using cloth is that injury to the covering is much less likely to occur, and can be very easily repaired with needle and thread, and the only disadvantage is that it takes longer to sew the cloth on than to paste or glue the paper. The cloth covers invariably fit better, and are efficient for a longer term of life.

The chief strain on the stick CD is backwards at C and D. (We are looking at the face of the kite.) In other words, the stick does not bend back at the point E or *between* E and D, and cannot do so whatever may be the wind pressure, for these reasons: The hanger, as shown, is attached to the upright stick at D and E, and the guy line ties in, as indicated. It will be seen that the upper portion of the hanger is the shorter, and since it is *always more in a direct line with the tension on the kite string*, the main pressure on the sticks comes at E. Sometimes the guy-line tension at D seems to be practically nothing. The pressure at the planes ACB and ADB contributes to this so much that it is wise to make the upright stick a little thicker for six inches above and below E. If AB is so flexible as to bend back in the wind sufficiently to alter the exposed surface much, then tie on an extra piece of the same thickness and about ⅔ the length of AB.

The second reason why both sticks at the point E should be stronger than elsewhere is that the lower planes AED and BED always form "bags" and at once bring a strain on the side strings AD and BD, which strain bends the upright back from the point E. The attachment of the hanger at the point E makes very little difference to the upright stick.

All this description is necessary in order to arrive intelligently at one of the weak points in kites of this description (single plane), and the one factor which gives so much trouble and is the cause of nine-tenths of the disasters to Malay kites; namely, the side strings *CADB* to which the covering is attached. In my own experience with something like forty kites, I have had only one stick break in the air, and that was the upright at the point E. All other sticks have been broken by carelessness in starting or landing the kite. The side strings, however, have certainly given trouble by stretching or breaking, developing a weakness which no one suspected for a long time. The importance of this weak point, I am ashamed to confess, I did not discover until my third year, although I had ample opportunity. Iron wire, steel wire, and very large cord have all given way under high strain before any other part of the same kite, and nothing has yet been found which brings the strength of this feature up to an equality as the others. It can be approximated sufficiently well for kites to be used in winds up to twenty-five miles by using twisted picture-cord of brass or iron.[1]

Kites of this description will fly without a tail, provided the kite balances along the line CED when held up by the finger at some point on the hanger. If either side is heavier than the other, tie a small piece of wood on the cross-stick until balance is secured; provided, also, that the planes above the cross-bar are properly proportioned (as above described in measurements) to those below. As long as these proportions are maintained, the kite flies; when they are disturbed by the stretching of any side string at any point, there is disaster in store. A very little stretching in a high wind will render the best kite useless, but may be tolerated in winds of low velocity, or even remedied for some time. The common symptom is best described by "sagging" — when the kite slowly sinks to the earth sideways. This is due to one of two causes: Either (1) the slight stretching of a side string in one of the lower planes (which, if considerable, results in diving); or (2) the undue flexibility of the cross-stick on the right or left of E. If due to the first, the kite sags to or towards the ground on the opposite side; if due to the second, it sags to or towards the ground on the same side — the reason being that the uppermost plane, which retains its original efficiency, dominates the other, which has become weaker, and forces it to the ground.

The remedy for stretching is to overhaul the side strings, and, by careful measuring, restore the proportions. The remedy for

---

([1] In speaking of a kite that will fly in a wind of twenty-five miles I mean one that will continue to do this on various occasions — not one that has been ruined on the trial.)

undue flexibility on either side of E is found in tying on a bracing-stick at the weak point, extending it a little beyond E. In most cases of fairly high winds the disturbance of "balance" of the two sides along the line of the upright may be disregarded, since the resistance to the pressure of the wind has been equalized, and it has been found that slight differences in balance are not noticed in high winds.

Darting about without diving to the ground means simply that the sticks are bending to the puffs, and, if the kite persists, the sticks must be braced by tying on extra pieces.

As regards tying the guy line on to the hanger: I have, in the past, obtained, from several directions, various measurements, and have found that all of them will work under certain conditions peculiar to certain kites. No rule can be given which will apply alike to all Malays. It depends upon the centre of gravity of the kite, which differs in each case, and upon the flexibility of the sticks. It is evident that, since the sticks bend in the wind, some more, some less, and that, since the upright stick bends backward at D, the angle made by the hanger and flying string will change as the point D moves. Therefore, since the angle changes, no rule can be given. The only sure way is to proceed as follows: Place the kite on the floor, face up. Try lifting it by the hanger at some point until you find a place which will raise all four of the ends of the sticks from the ground at the same time. Find ten per cent. of the distance to E from that point, and tie the guy line on at that point. If the kite will not rise, move the tying-point nearer E, one-quarter of an inch at a time, until the kite begins to dive. You are then too high. Moving the tying-point up or down less than one-quarter of an inch will frequently mend or mar matters. Once found, mark it with a colored thread and needle.

After the tying-on point has been once established, no further experiments in that direction will ever be necessary with that kite unless something happens to disturb the proportion between the areas above the cross-stick and those below it. Whenever that occurs (as by stretching of side strings — by far the most common cause) the remedy is to be found in over-hauling the edges, measuring and comparing the edges of one side with the other. Once corrected, the kite will fly again. Therefore, do not experiment with the tying-on point, when once satisfactorily fixed, in hopes of remedying any defects which the use of a kite develops.

As to size, the temptation to make larger and larger kites is quite natural, but kites not exceeding five feet are by far the most useful if one wishes to study kites and wind; if, however, flying for sport is paramount, then every one must find for himself the limit of size. It is only necessary to remember that a long stick is more flexible than a short one, and that stiffness rather than flexibility is what is wanted.

Those who wish to have a battle royal between a strong Malay and a small gale will find it advantageous to add another cross-stick as shown in the illustration. This stick stiffens the edges at the point where they are weakest, compels the kite to retain its shape, divides the pressure brought upon the upright stick by the side strings (always a great element of danger), and for these reasons makes the kite much more efficient in high winds. The illustration of the Malay represents a kite with which for nearly an hour I obtained in a wind of 35 miles a very remarkable record, but the kite was so badly stretched in doing it that I abandoned this form for very high winds and adopted the Hargrave. Still the experiment was very useful, and, in my opinion, all Malays intended for winds over 15 miles should be made that way. The cross-sticks and uprights were of spruce, 4 feet by ¾ inch by ½ inch, and lashed to them with small tarred marline were split bamboo sticks, one for each, of the same length. This gave me very heavy, but very stiff sticks. The side lines were of iron wire, No. 20, afterwards abandoned for blocking-cord, which, when shellacked, stretched but very little and broke at 75 pounds. Even this was none too strong. The cover was heavy cotton drill, and the complete structure weighed a little over 3 pounds. At an angle of 40° it pulled from 8 up to 48 pounds repeatedly — wind as above mentioned (35 miles) — and then unexpectedly dove and swooped to the right, carrying away two lightning rods on its way. Upon examination I found every measurement distorted, everything stretched out of shape, and nothing but a complete overhauling could make it fly again. The sticks were intact. It was merely a case of stretching all along the line until all those proportions upon which a good kite depends were lost. If any material can be found which will not stretch when cut on the diagonal, and which will not form too deep " bags " under heavy wind pressure, a kite of this plan could doubtless be made of great service, but it demands a very strong wind.

NOTE. — These experiments were conducted at Sharon, Mass., during the summers of 1892–95. Those described in the following article during August and September, 1895.

SOME EXPERIENCES WITH HARGRAVE KITES.

By J. B. Millet.

———————

After spending three summers in making, breaking, mending, and rebuilding Malay kites, always with an increasing enjoyment and accumulation of information, I found myself forced to the conclusion that Malays are not serviceable enough in winds from 15 miles an hour up. To be sure, they will fly in winds of 30 to 35 miles, and will frequently hold together for several severe trials on different occasions, but their efficiency in strong winds (20 to 35 miles) is much less than it should be in proportion to the exposed area. Moreover, this efficiency is rendered less trustworthy for scientific purposes, because, as the wind increases, a Malay nearly always develops eccentricities which are not apparent in a wind of less velocity; as, for example, darting from side to side, or "sagging," or sinking to the ground. Sooner or later, as the wind rises and becomes a small gale, something happens to make the kite practically useless, or which demands tinkering. Either the side strings stretch, or a stick breaks, or some stick bends too much, and so destroys the balance.

It was with considerable reluctance that I abandoned the Malay for use in high winds, and in the face of predictions that I would regret it, from kite-flyers whose knowledge, based on experience, I respect; but after having made and tested Hargraves, of very large and quite small dimensions, I reassert my belief in them with absolute confidence. I tested, on one occasion, a Malay weighing nearly 1 lb., having an area of 8 square feet, against a Hargrave weighing 1½ lbs., having a total area of a little less than 10 square feet, in a wind of 20 to 25 miles. The Malay, at an angle of 45–50 degrees, pulled from four to nine pounds; the Hargrave, at the same angle, pulled from

six to seventeen pounds. The lift is easily calculated. The
Hargrave was perfectly steady all the time, and required no
attention; whereas, the Malay, although in perfect condition,
needed more or less looking after nearly all the time.

This test was followed up by others almost daily, until from
a mass of results there was no escape from the conclusion that
the Hargrave was the steadier, the less likely to break or lose
its shape in the air, and — what is more important — lifted much
more per square foot of lifting-surface. What is needed is a
kite that can be anchored in the wind and left there without fear
of disaster from considerable increase in velocity, and that will
fly steadily and will not demand constant mending or balancing.

Such a kite I found the Hargrave to be. Its steadiness is
most remarkable — provided, of course, the kite is made with
care. After reading something of Hargrave's results, and with
his measurements in hand, one is tempted, quite naturally, to
try and improve on Hargrave's plan, either by altering the shape
of the " wings " or the position of the side planes which act as
fins to keep the kite in the eye of the wind. Doubtless some
improvements on Hargrave's best device will be made by such
experimentation, but in my opinion it is better to begin exactly
where Hargrave left off, and make your first superimposed
plane kite as exactly as possible on the proportions of his
measurements. Two kites of whatever plan, made as nearly
alike as possible, will no more act exactly alike than two cat-
boats made from the same model. Therefore it follows that the
disciple of Hargrave may, by using the same measurements,
be so fortunate as to excel the best efforts of the inventor himself. Experimenters with kites owe a large and rapidly increasing debt to Hargrave for this invention, and the least we can do
is to acknowledge it on all occasions. His kite is an absolute
departure from all previous forms, and is by far the most
efficient and durable; but it is not for very light winds. It demands winds of twelve to fifteen miles upwards, for although light
kites of this form can be made which will fly in winds of lower
velocity, they are too fragile to last. The form of the kite
demands stiffness both in sticks and covering, which quality
deserts us when we endeavor to introduce extreme lightness.

Plate XIII.

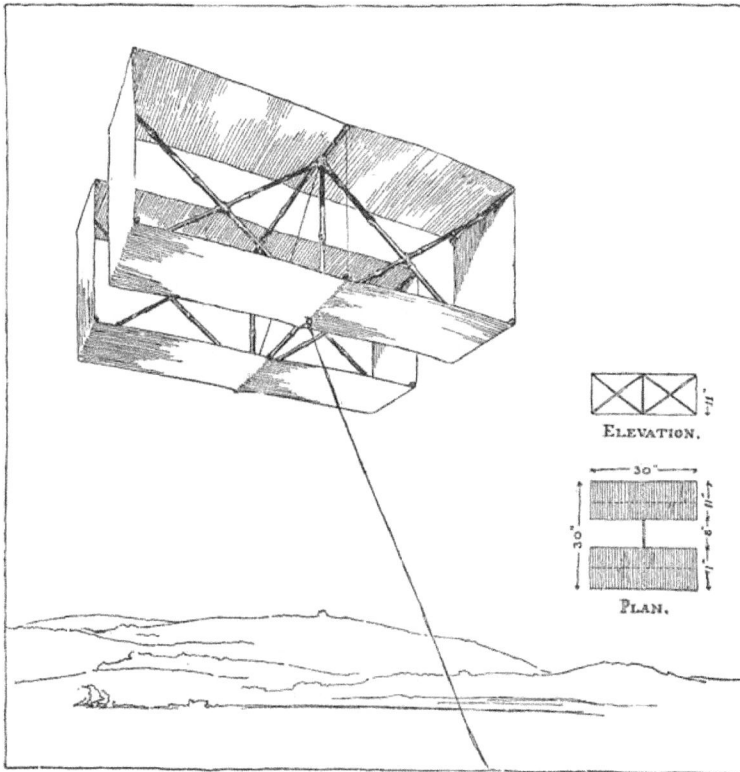

ELEVATION.

PLAN.

THE HARGRAVE KITE.

Drawn by an Expert.

Intentionally blank as was the original edition.

It will be found upon making a Hargrave that the time and labor spent are far greater than would be required to make several Malays; but in the end there is ample compensation, for the Hargrave does not require constant mending; the parts most frequently broken are very easily replaced; and the whole structure is neither thrown out of balance, nor does it require rebuilding. If the upright or cross stick of a Malay breaks, the repairing practically amounts to making a new kite. There is no breakage in a Hargrave which compares to this.

The thoroughly interested kite-flyer will supply himself with two or three Malays (say 4 or 5 feet tall) for light winds, and the same number of small Hargraves for heavier winds. In flying tandem they may be used together, and it will be found that the Malays are of great assistance in supporting the Hargraves in case the wind suddenly decreases below that velocity which the Hargraves require; whereas, if the wind increases beyond the point of efficiency for the Malays, they simply circle about or sag (as long as they hold together), and the Hargraves pay very little, if any, attention to them. In my opinion, therefore, a combination tandem team is the best one for most purposes, and especially whenever the wind is uncertain or likely to decrease. With the certainty of a heavy wind, a team of small Hargraves will give one or two active men their hands full. By small Hargraves I mean kites of the following dimensions, which I have found to be the most useful, all things considered. All mine were built on the proportions given by Mr. Hargrave in his published accounts, and varied in size from 8 feet spread and depth, down to 30 inches. The largest turned out to be practically useless, unless I had one or two men to assist, on account of its enormous strength. It was very difficult to find the exact point of attachment, because it could not be readily and safely controlled during experiments. The same proved true of all the others, down to what may be called the "three-foot limit." Here I found the most convenient and most useful size, the dimensions of which are given.

It has come to my knowledge that others beside myself were confused by the terms employed by Mr. Hargrave in referring to " height, depth, and width " of his kite. It was difficult to be sure of his meaning without constant reference; therefore I have in correspondence with others recommended the following terms: " Spread " means from tip to tip of the cell (just as in the case of a bird's wings), " depth " means distance from the front to the rear of any cell, while the length of the " main booms " gives the depth of both cells and the distance between added together, or extreme depth of the whole structure; " height" of a cell is, of course, the third and last dimension, and is, in fact, the height of the kite itself as it lies on the ground.

It will be found wise in three-foot cellular kites, or less, to depend entirely on lashings with waxed shoe-thread, and not to make any nail or screw holes. After the frame is put together before sewing in the cover, paint all the lashings with liquid glue, saturating them thoroughly. This adds very much to their strength and stiffness. My smallest kite is made in this way, and although it weighed but $1\frac{1}{4}$ pounds and exposed to the wind four planes (two in each cell) 30 $\times$ 11 inches, it safely out-weathered many severe blows (the highest exceeding 35 miles an hour) and is still in good order. The only break was one of the side sticks, which was repaired in a very few minutes. The cover has stretched some, but without affecting the flying qualities to any great extent. This kite, in a wind of 18 miles, up to 35, would easily carry a thermograph weighing three pounds. The best altitude for a period of thirty minutes maintained by this kite was 1,600 feet, with a wind of 18 miles. There was exactly 2,600 feet of large cord out (breaking at 100 pounds — far heavier and stronger than was needed, but no other was convenient), and the angle was greater than 45° for half an hour.

The best material for sticks is small stiff bamboo, while the cover can be made of very thin cotton cloth or percaline. After the cloth is on, and the kite has been found by trial to fly all right, the cloth should be thoroughly saturated with starch made up with benzine so that it will dry quickly. Do not use pressure, as you will be likely to stretch the covering. If put on with a wide brush it will cover evenly enough. It should be dried in the shade. When dry the cloth will be very stiff, and the bending back of the front edges (especially of the fins) will be very largely prevented; while the supporting planes will be much less likely to form pockets and thus increase the drift.

These kites often develop a tendency, especially when first flown, to "sag" down towards the ground to the right. Just why they sag to the right I am unable to say, but the fact is that every one I have made has always sagged to the right and never to the left, which is doubtless a coincidence, but may be due to something unknown to me. This sagging occurs before the cells have been adjusted; in other words, unless the kite flies all right, this sagging is most likely to be the cause. It means that the side of the kite nearest the ground is of weaker efficiency than the other, and is therefore borne down. In a gale which is beyond the strength of one of these kites, it yields to the pressure by "sagging" until it comes to the ground. This may be remedied, up to the limit of the strength of the materials used, by stiffening the weak sides. This is best done by bracing the string — carrying short pieces from one of the diagonals forward to some point on one of the booms. Try the rear cell first, as this particular weakness seems to be developed there oftener than in the front cell. If bracing with string does not remedy the trouble, hunt for a weak point in some diagonal or side stick on the side of the cell.

It will be found sometimes that the side stick bends under pressure, and tying on an extra piece (small, but quite stiff) outside of the cloth will often end the trouble. Once balanced, your troubles are fairly well over; for the kite may be depended upon to behave itself for a long time to come.

The selection of bamboo, the lashing of joints with waxed shoe-thread, and painting on a thick coating of liquid glue afterwards, proved to be most fortunate. The strength of this method of construction far exceeded my expectation, while the rigidity of the kite when flying in a wind of 30 to 35 miles was eminently satisfactory.

It will be noticed by reference to Plate XIII. that the spread and extreme depth (or length of the main booms) are but 30 inches, and the height 11. These dimensions are on so small a

scale as to make the kite appear *before trial* to be more of a
toy than a useful scientific structure, but my experience proves
that this size is by all means the most useful for all purposes
except the lifting of heavy weights. In order to try to lift a
man we could do no better than follow in Mr. Hargrave's foot-
steps, but when trying to reach as high an altitude as possible with, say, 3 pounds' weight (representing the thermograph), our problem is quite different. I have on several
occasions had this small kite out with 2,640 feet of cord, and
it frequently assumed an angle exceeding 55°, with very
little "bagging" of the string. In all cases I used string
twice as large and heavy as I otherwise would have, had not
the position of the kite been over a swamp several miles in
extent and I feared some unexpected break. Considering this
particular kite as in all respects the best one I had made or
seen, I was anxious to save it for a working basis. Regarding
it more as an experimental kite which I was quite prepared to
see blown to pieces, I did not use that care in the selection of
bamboo sticks which I would again. It is not difficult to
obtain sticks three feet long that are nearly the same diameter
throughout. The side sticks (one in each corner of each cell)
should be as stiff, but light, for if heavier than need be they
act as weights held out at the end of the diagonal sticks, and
bring an unnecessary strain on all the parts.

As regards fastening the guy line to the kite, the proper point
is in most cases near the rear edge of the forward cell, but the
centre of gravity of the kite determines this, and if this point
can be fixed a little forward of the edge the kite will take a
better angle. It will be found convenient to lash a small brass
ring at this point and fasten a small snap-hook on the end of
the guy line. Always hem both edges of the cloth and sew it
with a waxed thread wherever it touches the bamboo frame.
Measure every distance with care, so as to have right angles at
all the corners and no variation in the area of the cells. Special
care should be used to secure a balance of area and weight
along the line of the main booms, so that the areas on one side
will be exactly the same as on the other.

WORK ON THE GREAT DIAMOND.

By Charles H. Lamson.

HAVING an interest of long standing in aerial navigation and also incidentally in kites, when the 1895 April number of the " American Engineer and Railroad Journal " came to hand, describing Mr. Hargrave's latest box or cellular kites, I determined to make one. This kite, with some modifications of my own invention, has been about the most successful of any I have flown this year. The dimensions of my kite were as follows : Length of each cell, fore and aft, 25 inches, which was the full width of the black cambric cloth used for a covering. A narrow hem strengthened the selvage edge. Breadth of each cell, 6 feet, depth, 2 feet, distance between the cells, 4 feet 4 inches, making the full outside dimensions of the kite 6 feet wide and 8 feet 6 inches in length. Material of frame, straight-grained American spruce. The dimensions of the two strips constituting the backbone were $\frac{7}{8}$ by $\frac{1}{2}$ inch. The cross-braces for the cells were made elliptical in section, sharp edges exposed to the wind. Size of section, $\frac{7}{8}$ by $\frac{3}{8}$ inch. The outer corner pieces were tapered from the centre, one inch, to a quarter inch at the points. These were attached to the braces at the required angle by hinges of thin sheet brass. The other ends of the braces were simply notched to press against the corner of the backbone. This method was quite satisfactory. The two under pairs of braces were made four inches shorter than the ones that braced the upper corners, so as to give the cells a slight dihedral angle when placed in position for flight. This seems to me to be of some advantage in preserving the lateral stability of the kite. The cell frames were so made as to give the under sides of the covering a concave surface of $\frac{4}{8}$ of an inch in 25 inches. This kite having so much surface exposed to the wind, 50 square feet, was a very hard puller and uncomfortable to handle in a strong breeze. The writer therefore gave his attention to devising some arrangement whereby undue wind-pressure might be relieved and the kite flown with less danger of breaking away. To effect this purpose the two spars connecting the ends were cut near each cell and jointed so that the angle of the cells, in relation to each other and to the wind, could be changed at will. Two cords were used to limit and adjust this motion. The rear cell was weighted with a half pound of lead and the cells were rigidly fastened with both cells at an angle of about 10 degrees to the backbone. An extension or bowsprit, about 20 inches in length, was added to the lower side of the front cell, and the flying-string was then attached to the extreme point of same. This arrangement proved to be very successful, the pull immediately becoming so light that the cord could be held in the hand even in a high wind. Thus modified, the kite has never shown the slightest tendency to dive or to tip sidewise when flying, or when coming down after it has broken loose, always preserving an even keel and sailing away with a steady, majestic motion like a balloon, and landing softly on the ground without much injury to the kite. A neighbor and friend, Mr. Edward Rogers, becoming interested, was of material assistance in these experiments.

Our kite floating at a good angle with all our available string, we determined at a future trial to see if we could not let out a full mile. For this purpose I ordered from the Pawtucket Braided Line Company 6,000 ft. of No. 2 braided cotton fishline, which was furnished me without a knot, on a spool. After one or two attempts with insufficient wind, we at last had a perfect day for the test, the wind blowing steadily about 15 miles an hour. The loose edges of the kite shaking badly in the wind, they were stiffened by tacking in 8 thin, light spruce strips which we had provided for the purpose. Then getting our reel into position and bracing the cells in line, everything being in readiness we allowed the kite to go up. It sailed away like a soaring bird, and rose as rapidly as we could let out the

Plate *XIV.*

LAMSON'S MODIFIED HARGRAVE KITE.

For working drawings, see Plate XV.

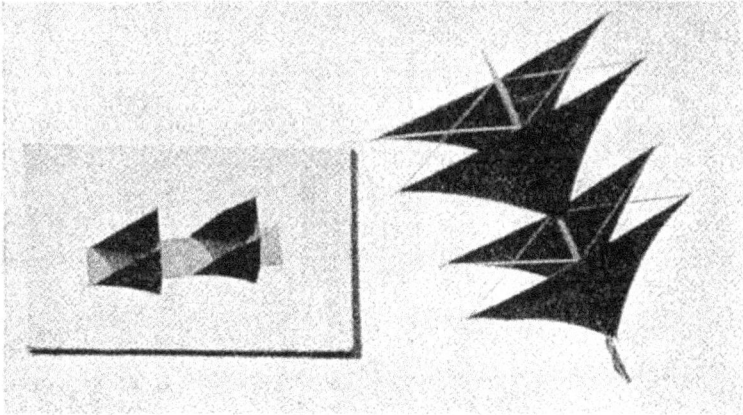

LAMSON'S MULTIPLANE FOLDING KITE.

The larger view shows the Kite being towed by a steamer. The smaller is a side view of the same Kite. Length, 12 feet; Width, 7 feet.

For working drawings, see Plate XVI.

Intentionally blank as was the original edition.

string. The large black boxes of the kite were nearly out of sight when it reached its full limit. After the 6,000 ft. was all reeled off it flew at an angle of about 40 degrees, and probably would have carried up more line if we had possessed it. For added safety a short piece of strong, elastic cord was sandwiched in next the kite. This event was much enjoyed by a large number of spectators, who assisted in winding in the cord. At no time was the pull so strong that the cord could not be easily held in the hand. This experiment took place at Great Diamond Island in Portland harbor, and after drawing in the kite to within about 300 feet of the ground, in order to test its capacity for being towed, we took our apparatus aboard the steamer homeward bound, with the kite still flying in the air. Taking our position on the deck, abaft the smoke-stack, we succeeded in making the roundabout trip to the city without any trouble; the steamer meanwhile turning to all points of the compass in making stops at her landings. We were able to go ashore at the city before hauling down the kite and closing our day's sport.

THE MULTIPLANE FOLDING-KITE. — Finding most kites rather troublesome to pack for transportation, the writer has invented a kite with triangular sails, having the frame jointed so that the sails can be folded back against a central keel. The sails are also adjustable in angle. There are eight of these sails superposed in pairs, two at each end of the keel, or backbone. The arms present sharp edges to the wind. The keel is also jointed at the centre. By folding the sails back, disjointing the keel, and putting the two parts side by side, a large kite can be slipped into a paper or cloth bag, making an unobtrusive package, easily carried under the arm. It is only a minute's work to set the kite up again, and it rises readily from the ground in a fair breeze. Little or no running is necessary to get it up. One of these kites, made of different-colored materials in cloth or paper, presents a most striking appearance in the air.[1]

---

[1] This kite being so complicated, it is hardly to be expected that many amateurs will care to take the trouble to make one, and, believing that the cause of aviation would be

HINTS TO KITE–FLYERS. — To avoid disaster, kite-flyers
should always select a large, level, clear space for their experiments, and away from any houses and trees, which create eddies
and currents very dangerous to kites. The seashore with a sea-
breeze is the ideal place. There are sometimes downward currents of air which may be avoided by a change of position, so, if
there is any wind, do not be discouraged if you do not get the
kite up the first time, but select a new spot and try again.
Have good cord of ample strength. Beware of hard-twisted
line. It winds up and kinks in damp weather. Sometimes
the line may be doubled to advantage. It is well to lay out
enough string so that the first start will bring the kite well above
any elevations in the neighborhood, and into a steady current
of air. Be careful to lay your string out exactly against the
wind, not across it. If a kite shows a tendency to dive, let out
quickly enough string to allow it to take a floating position, and
then it may be raised again, or it will come down to the ground
gently, when the cause of diving should be investigated. An
elastic cord next the kite end of the string is often an advantage
to prevent breakages in gusts. Court plaster is very convenient
for making quick repairs to the kite fabric.

In the writer's experience, large kites are more satisfactory
than small ones. Often a kite which would be very difficult to
fly, of the toy size, gives no trouble when made above six or
eight feet in diameter. It would seem that the larger surface
bridges the small pulsations of the atmosphere, and the added
weight tends also to stability. A toy boat tosses about on
the least ripple of the water, while a larger vessel would ride
steadily.

LILIENTHAL APPARATUS. — After a limited experience in
trying one of his soaring-machines, Lilienthal's apparatus seems

advanced by having them on sale, the writer has applied for a patent, and will have them
made for the market for the summer of 1896. It will be called Lamson's Multiplane Kite.
The writer has no objection to any experimenter making one of these kites for his own
use, should he prefer to do so. Address C. H. Lamson, 203 Middle Street, Portland,
Maine, U.S.A.

Plate XV.

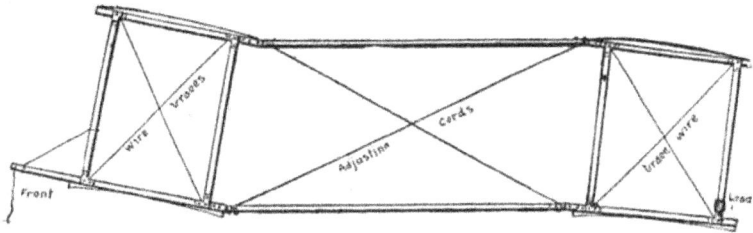

SIDE VIEW OF CENTRAL FRAME OR BACKBONE.

UNDER SIDE OF THE SAME.

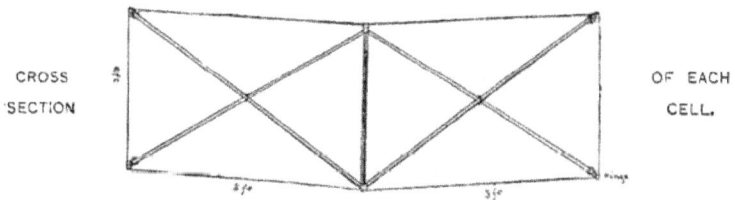

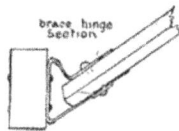

CROSS SECTION — OF EACH CELL.

brace hinge Section

Brace & Corner piece

Brace See

WORKING DRAWINGS OF LAMSON'S MODIFIED HARGRAVE KITE.

See perspective view in Plate XIV.

Intentionally blank as was the original edition.

Plate XVI.

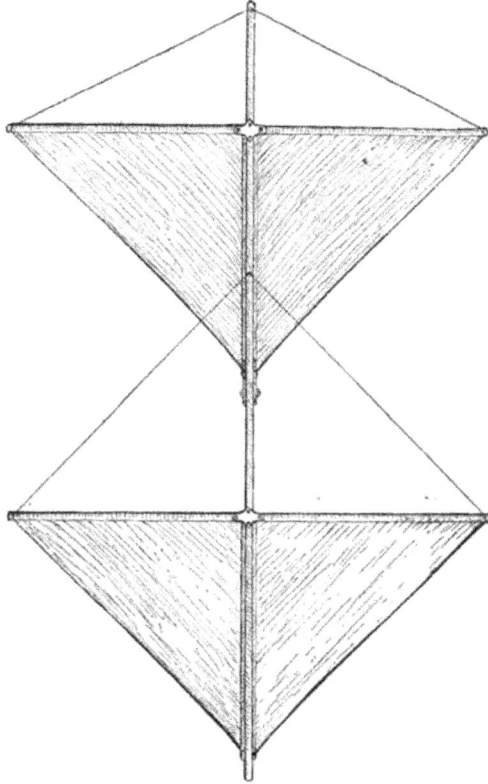

TOP OF KITE — OPENED.

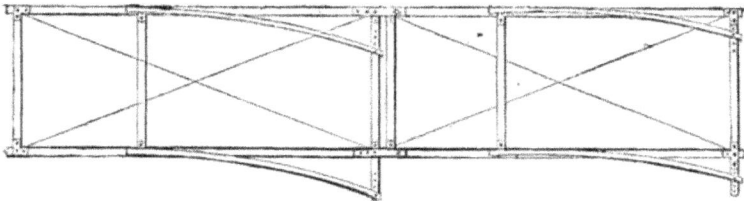

BACKBONE — SIDE VIEW.

WORKING DRAWINGS OF LAMSON'S MULTIPLANE FOLDING KITE.

See perspective view in Plate XIV.

Intentionally blank as was the original edition.

to the writer to have a number of serious defects.[1]   First, it is
too difficult of control for the average operator, when in the air.
Second, it has no elastic rear edges to assist in forward propulsion.   Third, the ribs and frame-work, as well as the body of
the operator, present a too large and too rough surface to the
air, impeding the necessary forward motion against the wind.
(A bicycle rider soon learns by experience what a powerful
effect even a moderate wind has in making his progress labo-
rious.)   In using the Lilienthal apparatus, the experimenter is
soon assured of the ample supporting effect of the air, but the
novice feels quite helpless to guide the machine.   It is also
very difficult to get a good send-off.   As Lilienthal says, " Confidence and skill must be acquired by *much* practice."

---

[1] At the time of writing, perhaps Mr. Lamson had not seen Lilienthal's latest design.
The next will probably be better, and so on.   *Sic itur ad astra.* — *Ed.*

MATERIALS USED IN KITE EXPERIMENTS AT BLUE HILL OBSERVATORY.

BY S. P. FERGUSSON.

ONE season of a few months is hardly sufficient for more than a beginning in the experimental study of kites, and the work at Blue Hill has consisted mainly of practical tests of materials used in the construction of kites. Some experiments have been made with four different types of kites, but the Malay or Eddy kite has so far received the most attention. The object of all the experiments has been to design a kite suitable for elevating meteorological instruments, and most of the kites made have been small and light, since the weight to be lifted is small. Hence, the conclusions set forth should be understood as concerning meteorological work rather more than aeronautical.

The essentials of a good kite are that its frame should be of strong, rigid material that is very light, and that the covering should be light, impervious to air, and smooth, so that the air may slide off the surface with very little friction; also, it should be made of material not liable to stretch while being used.

For frames both wood and metal are recommended, and for ordinary use in fine weather frames made of spruce are very satisfactory. Spruce is used almost exclusively at Blue Hill, care being taken to select straight-grained wood free from knots or other imperfections. Some experiments were made with umbrella ribs, but these were found to be less rigid and much heavier than spruce; also, much more time was necessary to construct the frame of umbrella ribs.

For covering kites both cloth and paper can be recommended. The advantages of paper coverings are their smooth, impervious surface, small liability to stretch, and the ease with which they

(138)

can be made or repaired.   Paper is not very durable, and is
very easily torn or punctured.   For covering the largest kites,
only tough paper, such as heavy manila or bond writing-paper,
should be used.   The bond paper is almost as strong as manila,
and is much lighter, though perhaps more easily punctured.
It is perhaps more expensive than other papers, but its advantages more than compensate for this, and it can be recommended
as one of the best materials for covering kites.   Cloth has the
advantage of being very durable, as it is not easily torn or punctured.   Its disadvantages are its liability to stretch, its rough
surface, and that it is not impervious to air.   The first defect
could perhaps be overcome by stretching the cloth before use,
and the other two defects by varnishing it, which renders the
surface both smooth and impervious to air.   Cloth is generally
heavier, and the best varieties for use, such as silk or nainsook
muslin, more than twice as expensive as paper.   It also requires more time for perparation than paper.   When experiments are made in rainy weather, or kites are sent up into clouds,
it is necessary to use cloth, because it is not injured by moisture.
As stated, silk and nainsook muslin gave the best results for
cloth kites at Blue Hill, though in large-sized kites unbleached
sheeting has also worked well.   Tracing-cloth appears to have
some advantages for covering kites, as it is very smooth, light,
and strong; but it is affected by moisture, which dissolves the
smooth varnish with which it is coated, and hence renders it
untrustworthy in rainy or wet weather.   Experience with both
paper and cloth coverings shows that with paper coverings the
angular height of the kite is much greater, and the lift, or " pull,"
upon the string also greater than in case of the cloth kites.
Kites covered with cloth are usually steadier than those covered
with paper.
    The best kind of cord for use in kite experiments is a close-
twisted linen line.   Shoe thread used for stitching soles is much
stronger than any other cord in proportion to its weight, but
being loosely twisted it is not nearly so durable as the close-
twisted cords.   Blocking-cord (used in blocking hats) is used
almost exclusively at Blue Hill.   This cord is of linen, and the

sizes range from Nos. 9 to 32, No. 9 being the smallest, with a
weight of about 5 oz. per 100 feet, and breaking at 75 to 90 lbs.
No. 12 breaks at 120 to 125 lbs. and weighs 6 oz. per 100 ft.;
No. 16 weighs 7 oz. per 100 feet, and breaks at 135 lbs.; No. 20
breaks at 155 lbs.; Nos. 28 and 32 did not break at 210 lbs.
(the limit of the testing scale). The weight of No. 32 is 13 oz.
per 100 feet. The cable-laid twines are also very good, the
largest size, No. 48, being about equal to No. 9 blocking-cord
in strength and durability. The cords described lose very little
of their strength after long use, unless they become abraded; and
are recommended as the best for general use. The success with
which pianoforte wire has been used in deep-sea sounding in-
dicates that it may be very useful in kite-flying when great
altitudes are desired. Single pieces of 5,000 feet or more in
length can be obtained, and the weight of wire capable of sustaining 200 lbs. is only one-half that of cord of the same
strength. A sample $\frac{3}{64}$ inch in diameter and 25 feet long did
not break with a strain of 210 lbs. This sample weighed 6 oz.
per 100 feet. The cost varies with different manufacturers, but
is generally nearly the same as that of cord of the same length.
In the use of wire, great care is necessary to prevent rusting,
which soon renders it useless; also, it must always be kept
under strain to prevent kinking. The success of experiments
depends greatly upon the condition of the line; and whether it
is of cord or wire, frequent inspection is necessary. Mr. Eddy
recommends, for safety, that all splices in the cord should be
replaced by knots, and that the average working-strain of the
line should not exceed one-fourth the breaking-strain of the cord
used. Experience at Blue Hill tends to confirm this. In joining
the ends of two cords the " surgeon's knot " alone should be
used, as there is then no danger of the line parting when under
variable strains.

SCREW PROPULSION BY FOOT-POWER.

By Samuel Cabot.

THE device I am constructing for propulsion by ariel screws is especially intended for utilizing the force of the legs as in the bicycle, but may be applied to the motion imparted by an explosion or steam motor, utilizing the reciprocating movement of the piston much as the push of the leg is applied to the treadle of a wheel. The machine is shown by a sketch in which GH represents an aeroplane fastened to upright hollow pipes

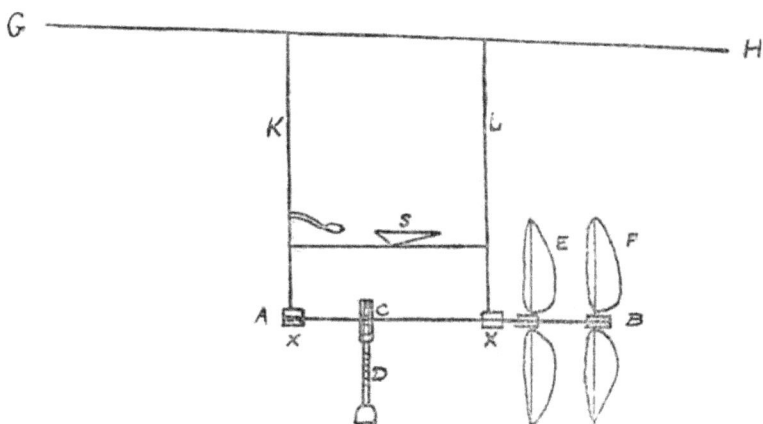

KL, at the bottoms of which are the ball-bearings XX, which carry in them the shaft AB. Upon the light shaft AB, preferably hollow, which lies in the direction of the propulsion desired, is rigidly fastened a sprocket wheel C, of as small dimensions as is compatible with the size of the shaft. Over this a sprocket chain D is passed, at each end of which a suitable stirrup is provided, into which the operator's foot is placed, the seat being shown at S.

It is now obvious that if the operator's feet are raised alternately straight up and down, the shaft will turn several revolutions to the right, and then an equal number to the left.

The two propellers or screws are placed behind the operator and close to the end of the shaft, but at a distance from each other at least as great as the width of the blades. These propellers are provided with two or more blades, and are of very light construction, but strong and stiff. They are of exactly the same construction except as to pitch, which is left on one and right on the other. They fit upon the shaft with suitable ball-bearings, allowing them to move around it very freely in one direction, but a friction clutch is so contrived that the left one is prevented from moving to the right, and the right one is in a similar manner prevented from moving to the left.

It will now be seen that at each push of one foot the shaft actuates one of these propellers, while the other continues to move in the opposite direction until its momentum from the last stroke of the opposite foot is exhausted. This exhaustion of the momentum, however, need not occur before the next stroke of the same foot comes and again adds to its momentum. The result is thus a constant or nearly constant motion of the propellers in opposite directions. As the pitches of the propellers are also opposed, the action upon the air is therefore constantly in one direction.

The objection to a single propeller, viz., its reaction, tending to turn the whole kite or aeroplane in the opposite direction, is obviated, as the reaction of the two propellers is equal and opposite, thus balancing each other. We thus have a single shaft oscillating by the action of the legs, much as in some of the old forms of bicycle, such as the "Star," and producing an almost constant motion of two propellers in opposite directions.

BIBLIOGRAPHY OF AERONAUTICS.

Continued from The Annual for 1895.

W. H. Kühl (*Jagerstr. 73. Berlin, W.* — Germany) has published a pamphlet of 50 pp., entitled *Aëronautische Bibliographie. 1670–1895.* Price 25 Pf. Important.

Congrès de l'Atmosphère, organisé sous les auspices de la Société royale de Géographie d'Anvers, 1894. Compte-rendu par le Chevalier Le Clément de Saint Marcq, Secrétaire Général. Anvers. Imprimerie Veuve de Backer, Rue Zirk, 35. 1895. Part VIII. of this report contains the following : *Contribution à la Bibliographie de la Locomotion Aérienne par Armand Wouwermans. I. Écrits primordiaux. II. Allemands. III. Anglais. IV. Français. V. Italiens, Espagnols, Portugais. VI. Néerlandais. VII. Scandinaves. VIII. Russes. IX. Collectifs, périodiques, etc. X. Accessoires.*

This is a very valuable contribution to the bibliography of aeronautics. The compiler's search has evidently been most careful and thorough. More than five hundred titles are given. The pamphlet contains 272 pp., of which 36 pp. are devoted to Part VIII. Price not given.

In the *American Engineer and Railroad Journal*, from October, 1894, to August, 1895, inclusive, there will be found under the heading " Recent Aeronautical Publications," a series of valuable lists. M. N. Forney, publisher, 47 Cedar street, New York.

The Annual Reports of The Aeronautical Society of Great Britain (Hamilton & Co., Paternoster row, London) contain lists of " Books, Pamphlets, etc., Received."

Zeitschrift für Luftschiffahrt. Monthly. Mayer and Müller, Berlin.

L'Aéronaute.   Monthly.   Paris, 91 Rue d'Amsterdam.

L'Aérophile.   Monthly.   Paris, 113 Boulevard Sébastopol.

Aeronautics.   Monthly.   Published from October, 1893, to September, 1894, inclusive.   Complete sets of 12 nos., $1.00. M. N. Forney, 47 Cedar street, New York.

Taschenbuch zum praktischen Gebrauch für Flugtechniker und Luftschiffer.   Edited by Capt. H. W. L. Moedebeck.   Published by W. H. Kühl, *Jagerstr. 73. Berlin, W.* — Germany.

Century Magazine, New York, January, 1895.   "A New Flying Machine," by Hiram S. Maxim.   This article should be read in connection with Mr. Maxim's article in this number of the Annual.

Harper's Young People, New York, January 29, 1895.   "The Building of Modern Wonders; the Flying Machine," by Hiram S. Maxim.

See list of works mentioned by Mr. Chanute on page 61 of this Annual.

Within the present limit of space, long lists cannot be given; the student who follows up the lines of search suggested above will find himself in the way of reading a very large amount of material.

There are two books which should be owned by every one who wishes to understand the aeronautical work which is now being carried on; they are:

"Progress in Flying Machines," by Octave Chanute.   Published by M. N. Forney, 47 Cedar street, New York, 1894. $2.50.

"Proceedings of the International Conference on Aerial Navigation."   Held in Chicago in connection with the World's Fair, Aug. 1, 2, 3, and 4, 1893.   pp. 429.   Published by M. N. Forney, 47 Cedar street, New York.   1894. $2.50.

To Publishers. — Aeronautical publications received will be noticed in future numbers of the Annual.

EDITORIAL.

Please address Communications to

THE EDITOR OF THE AERONAUTICAL ANNUAL,
BACK BAY P. O.,
BOSTON, MASS., U.S.A.

NOTE EXCEPTION. — From June 15 to Oct. 1, 1896, address:
YORK HARBOR,
MAINE, U.S.A.

Cable address: JASMEANS, BOSTON.

The publishers have remaining a few copies of the Annual for 1895. Price, postpaid, One Dollar.

TO ANTIQUARIAN BOOKSELLERS. — *The Editor is making a collection of old books, pamphlets, and prints relating to Aeronautics, and he will be glad to have quotations of prices of any such.*

EXPERIMENTERS IN ALL PARTS OF THE WORLD ARE INVITED TO SEND, FOR PUBLICATION IN THE NEXT NUMBER OF THE ANNUAL, CONCISE ACCOUNTS OF THEIR EXPERIMENTS.

Contributors will kindly note the following:

1. The Editor is not to be held responsible for rejected manuscripts, drawings, or photographs.

2. In describing experiments, contributors are requested to send photographs *and also* working-drawings of those pieces of apparatus which they consider their best.

3. Well-illustrated descriptions of experiments with the following kinds of apparatus are especially desired:

Soaring-machines.

Self-propelled models.

Kites.

Motors.

Screw-propellers.

4. All photographs should be distinct, or they cannot be satisfactorily reproduced. All drawings should be in ink on white paper or tracing-cloth, and they should be sufficiently well-executed to be photo-engraved without re-drawing.

5. Accuracy, explicitness, and conciseness of statement are desirable in the extreme.

6. Please state if any of the text or illustrations have been in print before, and, if so, where? Please give dates of all experiments.

It is expected that The Annual for 1897 will go to press on the first of October, 1896.

THE Editor wishes to express his indebtedness to the following members of the Boston Aeronautical Society, who, complying with his request, have kindly contributed articles to this number of The Annual. Prof. William H. Pickering, Messrs. A. Lawrence Rotch, J. B. Millet, Samuel Cabot, S. P. Fergusson, and Albert A. Merrill.

THE Editor is frequently asked, "What about Dr. Langley's recent experiments?" The only answer now to be made is, that Dr. Langley is not yet ready to give to the public the results of his recent researches.

Those students who are familiar with his memoir entitled "Experiments in Aerodynamics" are aware that it is his custom to complete a series of experiments before publishing results. If fragmentary reports had been made of his work prior to 1891 they would not have been understood.

When Dr. Langley had worked out his conclusions, he gave them all to the public.

The reports of his work which have appeared in the public prints during the past year or two have been unauthorized and misleading.

It is hardly worth while for a student to attach any importance to what is printed concerning the details of Dr. Langley's experiments unless the same is printed over his own signature.

THE MASTER OF SOME SAILING-SHIP will confer a great favor if he will bring home in good condition the skins of one or two of the very largest albatrosses. The birds should be most carefully weighed as soon as killed, and each skin should bear a tag giving this weight. If measurements are made before the birds are cold, giving the distance from tip to tip of the wings when fully extended, and also of the distance from the ends of the beaks to the ends of the tails, also of the greatest girth of the skinned body, these will be a great aid to the taxidermist who mounts the skins. These specimens are much needed. Perhaps the " Ancient Mariner " would not have come to grief if the albatross had been killed in the cause of science.

MOTORS. — At the close of an article in the " North American Review " of October, 1895, Mr. Maxim says, " My experiments during the last five years have led me to believe that the flight of man is possible, even with a steam-engine and boiler. I would, however, advise the young engineers who may read this paper, if they wish to do something to advance the science of aviation, to turn their thoughts in the direction of a petroleum motor. These motors have been greatly improved of late years, and I believe it is to the petroleum motor that we must look in the future, as being the engine which will drive our flying-machines. Petroleum is cheap and abundant; it may be obtained in any quarter of the globe, and no other substance that we can obtain on a commercial scale contains such an enormous quantity of latent energy."

When we consider Mr. Maxim's engineering skill, and when we remember how elaborate, we may almost say how exhaustive, have been his experiments with steam motors, we see how weighty are these words of commendation which he gives to the petroleum motor. This advice to young engineers is most generously given; it has cost him large sums of money and years of deep study to qualify himself to give it, and it should be valued accordingly.

For some time past the Editor has been gathering information concerning the gasoline and petroleum motors now on the market. Just at present the market seems to be in a state of preparation.

The interest in automobile vehicles which has recently been awakened bids fair to result in the development of light motors. For this reason the students of aeronautics are likely to take much interest in the development of the horseless carriage.

The recent speed-trials in France and in this country show that the carriage-builders are coming forward promptly with their energy and their money; also that the motor-makers have only partially solved the problem of producing a light motor. The full solution, however, is perhaps not far off.

The Editor wishes to obtain for his own use a motor which can lift 550 lbs. at the rate of 4 feet per second; the four-horse-power motor of commerce cannot always do this. Information concerning the exact weight, size, and price of a motor which can do it will be gladly received.

FLAPPING WINGS vs. SCREW PROPELLERS. — There is a difference of opinion as to which is the best method of propelling a flying-machine, — by flapping wings or by screw propellers. The evidence so far gathered seems to show that the latter method is the more rational of the two. The difficulty of preserving the equilibrium is thought by many to be increased by having movable wings.

With sustaining surfaces, which in the course of flight do not change their position relatively to each other, soarers have often been made which are self-righting; that is, they steer themselves into a course which is approximately horizontal.

There are still other reasons why screw propulsion seems to be the best. These were mentioned in an article which the present writer contributed to the "Boston Transcript" of January 12, 1884, and from which the following is an extract:

"Too close an imitation of nature is in many cases more of a hindrance than an aid. To illustrate this point . . . let us suppose the world to have wanted a locomotive. If the inventor had looked to nature for his model, he would probably have chosen, as being the most powerful, the elephant. Then, if he followed the method of those who are trying to solve our difficulty by a study of wing movements, he would have constructed a vast machine with legs and levers!

" Or, again, suppose the inventor who wished to propel a ship by its own motive power should have sought to apply that power in the same manner that nature applies it; he would have gone to the duck, and the product of his thought would have been a web-footed ship!

" It is quite right for us to study nature that we may learn principles; but, as has been said, if we attempt to make the same application of power we do not progress.

" In mechanics we find that the form of power which can be most readily utilized is rotary; . . . but in the animal world revolution is unknown; all propelling power, whether of beast, bird, or fish, is applied by oscillatory movement. The reason for this is not far to seek. Living creatures are dependent upon the circulation of the blood. Revolution necessitates the existence of an independent revolving body."

———

THE AUSTRALIAN KITE-DESIGNER. — For many years Mr. Lawrence Hargrave, of New South Wales, has been experimenting with flying-models and with kites. His work has awakened a great deal of interest among the students of aeronautics, and every new report of his experiments finds eager readers. Those who are unfamiliar with Mr. Hargrave's studies will find interesting accounts in Mr. Chanute's " Progress in Flying Machines," pp. 218–233, and in the " Proceedings of the International Conference on Aerial Navigation," pp. 287–297.

He has read several papers before the Royal Society of New South Wales. These may be found in the Journal of that Society. He says that copies are in the following libraries in Boston: American Academy of Arts and Sciences, Boston

Society of Natural History, State Library of Massachusetts,
" and in sixty-five other libraries in the United States."

In one of his later papers, read June 5, 1895, Mr. Hargrave
writes:

" The cellular kite is the germ that has been modified and
developed, and in all probability it will prove to be the perma-
nent type of the supporting surfaces of flying-machines. A
single experiment will show any one that absolute stability and
certainty of action may be relied on, and that the careful
adjustment and balancing of single planes and affairs with a
diedral angle is wasted labor.

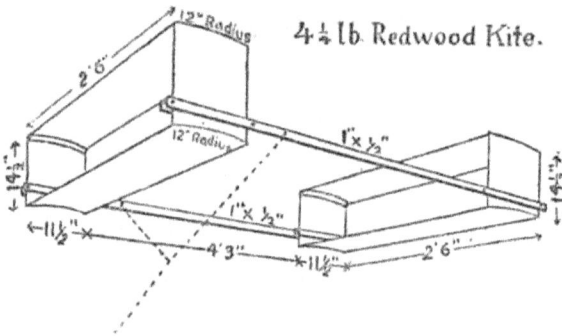

4¼ lb. Redwood Kite.

" The earlier forms of cellular kites had the planes alto-
gether edged with wood, and they needed much diagonal stay-
ing. Pin and eye joints would have been necessary at all the
corners if they had been made to collapse, and want of space
for storage began to be felt. The distance between the cells
has been greatly reduced; the exact distance that they can
be apart without impairing the efficiency of the after-cell is
not known; but, as far as stability is concerned, a single cell
is in stable equilibrium. There is a single-celled kite in the collection, measuring 2 ft. 6 in. long, 2 ft. 6 in. deep, and 6 feet
wide, and it flies quite steadily.

" A number of experiments have been made with curved
wooden cellular kites."

Mr. Hargrave speaks of the kite shown in the accompanying

drawing as one of a variety of stable forms, and he thinks it may be useful to his readers. Of this there can be no doubt.

The experiments which Mr. Millet has made, and which are described in his article, are sure to arouse the enthusiasm of kite-flyers, and to lead many to test the Hargrave kite. Mr. Millet has often said that he considers the Australian a far more advanced kite-designer than any other whose experiments have been reported.

Further light upon the Hargrave kite is thrown by Mr. Lamson, who has experimented with it and modified it as described on preceding pages.

In the last pamphlet which Mr. Hargrave sent to The Annual was the following table, containing the dimensions of five cellular kites similar to those described by Mr. Millet. Although this table has already been published by "The American Engineer and Railroad Journal," it is so sure to be useful that it is here appended:

Kite.	Length of each cell.	Breadth of each cell.	Depth of each cell.	Distance between the cells.	Distance from the forward end of the forward cell to the point of attachment of the kite string.	Weight of the kite.	Lifting surface of the kite.
A . .	1 ft. 11 in.	5 ft. 0 in.	1 ft, 10 ⅛ in.	2 ft. 1 in.	1 ft. 7 in.	5 lbs. 7 oz.	38.5 sq. ft.
B . .	1 " 11 "	5 " 0 "	1 " 10½ "	2 " 4 "	1 " 7 "	5 " 14 "	38.5 "
C . .	2 " 3 "	7 " 8 "	1 " 10¼ "	4 " 5 "	2 " 8 "	9 " 8 "	69 "
D . .	2 " 6 "	6 " 6 "	2 " 3½ "	3 " 6 "	2 " 3 "	9 " 0 "	65 "
E . .	2 " 6 "	9 " 0 "	2 " 6 "	4 " 0 "	2 " 10 "	14 " 8 "	90 "

THE TAILLESS KITE. — Mr. William A. Eddy, of Bayonne, N.J., was one of the first men in this country to give serious attention to the development of the kite. For several years he has advocated its use for the exploration of the upper air.

For the past two summers Mr. A. Lawrence Rotch, the

founder and director of the Blue Hill Observatory, has made it possible for Mr. Eddy to experiment in this direction.

The Blue Hill kite-experiments have awakened much interest.

Mr. Chanute writes of Mr. Eddy as follows: " He has been constantly experimenting with kites during the last few years, and he is recognized as an expert in such matters."

Mr. Eddy had one convex kite in his collection at Blue Hill last summer which he called the " Beard Kite," and which is described in Mr. Daniel C. Beard's " The American Boy's Handy Book" (published by C. Scribner's Sons, N.Y.).

Mr. Beard has given to kite-flyers the earliest working-drawing of a tailless kite, such as is now called the Malay, which the editor has so far found.   The description is given in an unsigned letter, dated Rochester, N.Y., Jan. 6, 1882, and is to be found on pp. 384–386 of the 1893 edition of the book just mentioned.

Mr. Eddy's modification of the tailless kite is known as the Eddy kite ; it has been tried by many experimenters who have worked from drawings furnished by the designer.   The accounts of Mr. Eddy's experiments which have been published from time to time during the past few years have done much to awaken an interest in kite-designing.

Complying with a request made by the Editor, Mr. Eddy writes :

To the Editor of the Aeronautical Annual:

The following is the best Eddy kite for winds above 6 miles per hour, for the season of 1895.   Upright and cross sticks of equal length.   See Fig. 1.

$$AC = BD.$$

BD and AC, 60 inches each.

Spruce sticks, $\frac{5}{16} \times \frac{7}{16}$ inch.

$$BE = 18\% \text{ of BD.}$$

The cross-stick AC (see Fig. 2) is bowed to a curve in which FG (to the deepest part of the bend) is 10% of AC, or six inches.   The string extending from S to E (Fig. 3) is of a length corresponding to the distance around the curved face of the kite from E to A.   Therefore, the distance SD corresponds to DA.   The distances, however, are never exact, since the point S, or rather the knot at S, should be shifted up and down in the wind to the extent of an inch or two, or until experiment has decided the true position.

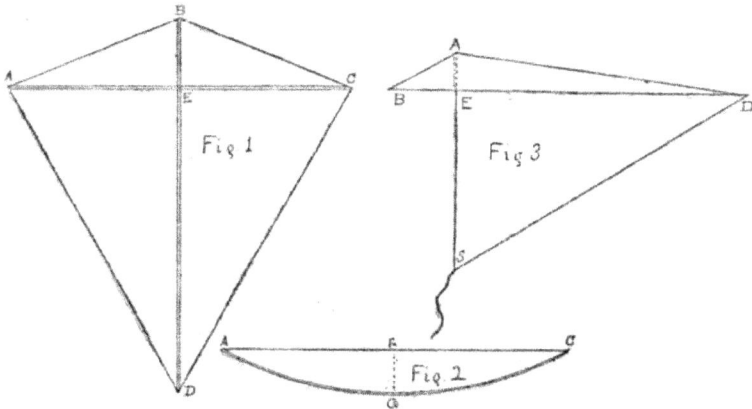

Fig 1

Fig 3

Fig 2

For winds of 3 to 6 miles an hour AC should be 14% of BD longer than BD, and spruce sticks $\frac{1}{4} \times \frac{3}{8}$ inch should be used.

Cloth should be used for all kites exceeding six feet in diameter.   The best calm-wind flyers are of paper, which is lighter than cloth.   Every fraction of an ounce in weight counts heavily in very light winds.

Nine Eddy kites produced a pull of 115 lbs. at Blue Hill Observatory; viz., three kites 9 ft., three 6 ft., one 7 ft., and two 5 ft. in diameter.   An altitude of about 3,000 feet was reached by the top kite.   Sixty-five mid-air photographs have been taken and printed.

WILLIAM A. EDDY.

THE following is a copy of the earlier bill referred to in the article entitled *Senate Bill No. 302* :

A BILL TO SECURE AERIAL NAVIGATION.

S. 1344. Fifty-third Congress, 3d Session. Introduced in the Senate of the United States by Mr. Cockrell, Dec. 20, 1893. Referred to the Committee on Interstate Commerce. Reported by Mr. Brice without recommendation, Feb. 25, 1895.

Be it enacted by the Senate and House of Representatives of the United States of America in Congress assembled, That the Secretary of the Treasury is hereby authorized and directed to pay the sum of one hundred thousand dollars to any inventor, from whatever part of the world, who shall, at any time prior to the first day of January, nineteen hundred, construct a vessel that will, on the verified report of three engineers appointed by the Secretary of War, demonstrate, within or near the city of Washington, the practicability of safely navigating the air at a speed of not less than thirty miles an hour, and capable of carrying passengers and freight weighing a total of at least five tons.

KITE-FLYERS WHO COMPETE FOR PRIZE C, mentioned on page 87, *may* find it necessary to design kites which will spill the wind when gusts come. Here are two hints: (1) See page 196, lines 13–18, of Mr. Chanute's " Progress in Flying Machines." (2) Consider valvular surfaces.

THE WEAKEST PLACE in a kite string is usually found in a knot. Some knots are better than others, but all are bad. There must be some joining. This one is better than any knot: RR, two thimble-rings. M, a link of steel wire. SS, two ends of a kite string served with soft waxed thread. Before passing the string around the rings, protect it with a strip of kid; let the kid run under the serving. Knots are more easily made, and some kite-flyers prefer them until they have lost a few miles of good line.

A SIMPLE instrument for measuring the angle at which a kite flies may be made with the following materials: A piece of pine board 16 in. × 5 in. × ½ in., two screw eyes such as are used in the backs of picture-frames, a weight of two or three ounces, and a piece of string. Screw the eyes into the upper edge of the board near the ends; these are for sights. Near what we may call the muzzle sight, make on the board a graduated quadrant. Drive a small nail at the centre of this quadrant, and attach the string, which is to be weighted at its lower end. Look through the sights at the horizon and see that the string hangs at zero on the quadrant. Cut away enough wood so that the string may hang at 90° when the sights point to the zenith.

When a kite is observed through the sights, the string will show the angular altitude on the quadrant.

———

A REEL about a foot in diameter, fitted with a brake and screwed to a wheel-barrow, is useful to the flyer of kites.

In high winds he needs a mallet, some stakes, and a lashing, lest the barrow make leeway.

———

IF you make kites, you will find a constant use for spruce sticks. Clear and straight-grained spruce is surprisingly strong. On no account touch anything but the finest quality. At the beginning of the season you can easily have some boards sawed into strips such as you need, and if you are thus supplied much time will be saved.

———

SAID Mrs. Lecks to Mrs. Aleshine, " Black stockings for sharks." It's a poor rule that won't work any way you want it to, therefore it may be added, *Black cloth for kites*. You can see a black hawk farther than you can a white swan. Think, too, of the sensitive plate which is the retina of the camera.

DURING the season of 1895 so much time was given to kites that I have not been able to carry my soaring-machine experiments[1] as far as I had hoped to do.

The experiments which I have tried, however, lead me to think that the most successful machine of the future will have its length fore and aft at least double, perhaps treble, that of the width measured from tip to tip of the wings or sustaining surfaces.

One experiment which I intended to make I have not yet found time for. I hope that some one may be interested to try it. It is to set a kite in free flight as a soarer. A long kite like the one in Plate XII. will, perhaps, answer the purpose for the first trial. A weight should be arranged to slide upon a rod or cord underneath the kite and parallel with the back-bone. This weight at first should be placed a little forward of the centre of the middle kite; there it should be tied. A strong rubber band should be attached to it and tightly stretched to pull the weight forward when it is released. Before the kite is sent up a lighted slow-match should be placed so that it will release the weight and cut the kite-line at the same time. This sets the kite in free flight, and as the rubber pulls the weight forward the centre of gravity is changed, and the kite may thus be properly ballasted as a soarer.

As improvements are made in kites from year to year, repeated trials of this experiment are likely to be instructive.

IN my experiments at York, Me., last summer, I was fortunate in having the assistance of Mr. Charles W. Bowles, of Canton, Mass. His skill in constructing kites is only equalled by his patience in experimenting with them.

A FLYING kite does not necessarily show the direction of the wind, *i.e.*, a kite does not necessarily fly dead to leeward of the place where the string is held. When several kites are flown from the same point, they will often bear in different direc-

[1] See the Annual for 1895, pp. 152-167 inclusive.

tions. If the divergence is great, it is probably due to lack of bilateral symmetry in some or all of the kites, although variations in wind currents cause some divergence.

IF a kite is unsteady in its flight, it does not *necessarily* follow that it is not well designed and constructed. A study of air currents will help the kite-flyer to understand the movements of his kite.

Most eccentricities of kite-flight are the effects of one of these three causes:

(1) Irregularity of the wind.

(2) Distortion of the kite.

(3) Faulty designing.

SPEEDS IN MILES PER HOUR REDUCED TO FEET AND METERS PER SECOND.

---

5 miles per hour	=	7⅓ ft. per sec.	=	2.235 meters.
10 " " "	=	14⅔ " " "	=	4.470 "
15 " " "	=	21⅔ " " "	=	6.705 "
20 " " "	=	29⅓ " " "	=	8.941 "
25 " " "	=	36⅔ " " "	=	11.176 "
30 " " "	=	44 " " "	=	13.411 "
35 " " "	=	51⅓ " " "	=	15.646 "
40 " " "	=	58⅔ " " "	=	17.882 "
45 " " "	=	66 " " "	=	20.117 "
50 " " "	=	73⅓ " " "	=	22.352 "
55 " " "	=	80⅔ " " "	=	24.587 "
60 " " "	=	88 " " "	=	26.822 "
70 " " "	=	102⅔ " " "	=	31.293 "
80 " " "	=	117⅓ " " "	=	35.763 "
90 " " "	=	132 " " "	=	40.234 "
100 " " "	=	146⅔ " " "	=	44.704 "

INDEX EXPURGATORIUS.

For the Use of Young Writers.

DÆDALUS.

ICARUS.

PHAETON.

PEGASUS (admissible pictorially).

D. GREEN.

NATIONS' AIRY NAVIES.

PILOTS OF THE PURPLE TWILIGHT.

INTREPID AERONAUT.

(*To be continued.*)

LILIENTHAL may learn from Maxim that a long fore and aft dimension is desirable.

Maxim may learn from Lilienthal that one must "feel at home with the wind" before he can steer a flying-machine.

Lilienthal may learn from Maxim that propulsion by screws is more rational than propulsion by flaps.

Maxim may learn from Lilienthal that it is better to experiment with machines just large enough to carry the operator than it is to build machines weighing several tons.

What perhaps might be the quickest method of bringing about the full solution of the problem of aerial navigation is one which, under free government, is not workable.

If Lilienthal and Maxim, each of whom possesses qualifications which the other lacks, were together exiled to a lonely island in the South Seas, with a goodly company of artisans, an ample commissariat, and plenty of material, machines, tools, and fuel, and then if their ships were burned and they were told to fly home — but I pause, — the Annual isn't a novel: it is a very serious publication, and prithee remember that it *is* an Annual, and that another number will be asking your kind attention about twelve months hence.   Till then, adieu.

www.ingramcontent.com/pod-product-compliance
Lightning Source LLC
Chambersburg PA
CBHW031258090426
42742CB00007B/507